QUESTIONS
and
ANSWERS
for
TODAY'S CATHOLIC

Other Books by Michael Manning

Pardon My Lenten Smile

Proclaimed from the Rooftops

On Camera and Off

QUESTIONS

AND

ANSWERS

FOR

TODAY'S CATHOLIC

A Catholic Answers
Difficult Questions

Father
Michael Manning, SVD

Thomas Nelson Publishers
Nashville, Tennessee

Imprimi Potest
Very Reverend Joseph Miller, SVD
Provincial
Reverend Alfonse Zimmerman, SVD
Censor Deputatus

Published in Nashville, Tennessee, by Thomas
Nelson, Inc.

Scripture quotations are from THE REVISED
NEW AMERICAN BIBLE. Copyright © 1988,
Thomas Nelson, Inc., Publishers.

Library of Congress Cataloging-in-Publication Data

Manning, Michael, 1940–
      Questions and answers for today's Catholic / Michael Manning.
         p.   cm.
      Includes index.
      ISBN 0-8407-7450-8
      1. Catholic Church—Miscellanea.   I. Title.
BX1754.3.M24   1990   90-38748
282—dc20   CIP

Printed in the United States of America
2 3 4 5 6 7 - 95 94 93

To my Brothers
in the
Divine Word

CONTENTS

Acknowledgments

Introduction

SECTION 1
The Struggles We Share 35

How can I find God's will for me?

Why am I not happy?

Is it a sin to feel inferior?

My faith seems to be stagnating. How can I grow spiritually?

How should I handle negative feelings?

Why is patience important?

How can I keep from feeling discouraged?

How can I recover from being hurt by a loved one?

What if the person who has hurt me doesn't think his action requires forgiveness?

Because my father was an alcoholic, I'm having problems as an adult. Should I just pray, or can I do something else?

Why is trust difficult for me?

Does God answer all prayers?

How do I find time for proper prayer?

The Bible

Why don't Catholics stress reading the Bible more?

How did Catholic reluctance to read the Bible begin?

Isn't the written Word all we need of God's revelation? Why do Catholics also need tradition?

How do we assess those oral traditions that aren't explicitly found in the Scriptures?

What do Catholics believe about tradition?

As a Catholic, I have never read the Bible. Can you make this book less intimidating to me?

Where should a Catholic start reading the Bible?

What's the difference between the Catholic and Protestant Bibles?

Why is the Catholic Church against a literal interpretation of Scripture?

Would you encourage a Catholic who wants to go to a nondenominational Bible study?

Jesus

Do Catholics "know" Jesus?

How do you personally respond to the question, "Do you know Jesus?"

Do Catholics believe that Jesus is God and man?

Why do Catholics talk about doctrine so much? Why not just talk about Jesus?

Jesus often criticized the Pharisees for their legalism, yet you Catholics seem to have laws for just about everything, don't you?

Worship

What is the "Mass" that Catholics go to on Sundays?

What is this sign of the cross that Catholics make over themselves?

Is it okay for a Catholic to go to a different parish or denomination that suits her better?

So much for the ideal. Now get realistic. What happens when, no matter how hard you try, over a long period of time you find nothing but antagonism or a lack of spiritual nourishment?

How can I change my "dead" parish?

What would a Catholic find if he/she decided to come back to church after many years away? Wouldn't he/she be uncomfortable?

Why do so many Catholics not go to church?

I don't go to church because I don't want to be a hypocrite. I'm not going to pretend I'm a saint like all those "holier-than-thou" people.

Sometimes I wonder if most Catholics are just nominal Christians.

Catholics seem to be proud of having so many members. Is it a blessing to be part of such a large and often impersonal organization?

Why can't Mass be said in Latin?

Is our society losing touch with the sacred?

If Saturday is the Lord's day, why do Catholics worship on Sunday?

Why do priests wear elaborate vestments in church when Jesus wore such simple clothes?

Why do Catholic churches have statues? Scripture is clear about "no graven images."

Do Catholics believe in fasting?

Mary, Saints, and Angels

What is the meaning of the Catholic practice of
canonizing saints?

What is this apparition of Mary at Fatima that
some Catholics are so excited about?

Do Catholics have to believe in such apparitions
of Mary?

Why do Catholics give so much attention to
Mary, the mother of Jesus? She often seems to
get more attention than her Son.

Why did Catholics begin to venerate Mary?

I can't see Mary as anything more than a fine
example from the past. Catholics act as if she's
still alive.

Now wait a minute. Scripture says that there is
only one mediator—Jesus!

I don't like the idea of relationships with spirits.
Isn't it unbiblical?

I get the image of King Saul conjuring up evil
spirits with the witches of Endor.

This is foreign to me. I still have problems with
others getting in the way of my direct
relationship with the Lord.

What is the rosary?

Now, I think you are definitely going against
Jesus when you pray with such repetition.
Jesus warns against such rattling on in
Matthew 6:7.

Do you believe that Mary was always a virgin? In
my Bible Jesus has brothers and sisters.

The assumption of the blessed Virgin Mary is hard for me to accept. Do Catholics believe she is some goddess?

Do Catholics believe in guardian angels?

Satan

What do you know about the devil?

What about demon possession?

Religious Communities

What are religious communities like the Jesuits, Benedictines, and Franciscans?

What about these contemplative Catholics who close themselves off from the world to pray?

What are the vows of poverty, chastity, and obedience that members of these communities take?

Please explain more about the vows.

Isn't it very difficult to choose a life of celibacy?

Jesus says I should leave everything and follow Him. I don't understand such surrender.

Am I disqualified from being a Christian because I have a car, a house, and credit cards? Should I forget about my wife and children's needs?

Wrestling with God

How can you say God is loving when there are so many tragedies in our lives?

If you watched someone you love very much writhing to death with the constant pain of vaginal cancer, would you honestly look to the Source of life and the Sustainer of creation with love?

Will I ever be able to find God as loving in the midst of my anger and loss?

The End Times

Do Catholics believe in the second coming of Jesus?

Do Catholics believe in the Antichrist?

Is the Roman Catholic Church the Antichrist?

Why do some people use the book of Revelation (Apocalypse) to scare people into coming to God?

SECTION 3
The Seven Sacraments 115

What are these Seven Sacraments that seem so important to Catholics?

Are the sacraments based on Scripture or tradition or both?

Baptism

Why do Catholics baptize infants?

What is "original sin"?

What is this "limbo" you Catholics believe unbaptized babies go to?

Why would a priest refuse to baptize a child because the parents weren't married in the church or aren't active in the parish?

Confirmation and the Holy Spirit

What is the Charismatic Renewal?

Does the Catholic Church recognize the experience of being "filled with the Holy Spirit"?

Do Catholics believe in the gifts of the Holy Spirit?

What is the gift of tongues?

Reconciliation

What is confession?

Don't Catholics go to confession in some dark box?

Do Catholics go to confession so that they can be free to sin again?

Why do Catholics have to confess their sins to a man and not directly to God?

Sin

What can I do about the sin of resentment?

Why do we have temptations?

I don't seem to have the willpower to turn away from a particular sin. What should I do?

What should I do about past sins that bother me?

I'm having problems with scruples.

What is the sin against the Holy Spirit that can never be forgiven?

Are my sins mortal or venial?

You mentioned not eating meat on Friday. Has that restriction been changed?

I have done many bad things in my life. Can God forgive me?

Why do I feel guilty?

Is doubting God a sin?

Eucharist

Is Jesus really present in the Eucharist?

That's very nice and even inspiring. But don't Catholics get so involved in Holy Communion that they fail to see Christ in others?

Why do Catholics receive only the bread at Mass while the priest also drinks the wine?

What about Catholics who are excluded from receiving Communion because of sin?

I am divorced, but I want to receive the sacraments. What should I do?

Family and Marriage

My marriage is on the rocks. How can I bring new life into it?

Is it wrong not to want children in our marriage?

Why is it so difficult to be married in the Catholic Church?

What do Catholics think about wives being submissive?

Since Jesus says to "turn the other cheek," should I stay with a husband who abuses me and my children?

I am afraid to discipline my children. What do you suggest?

Is it possible to have a happy marriage if the spouses belong to different religious denominations?

Should a couple marry because the woman is pregnant?

In a world where divorce is so common, I refuse to marry before I live with my boyfriend.

Do Catholics believe in divorce and remarriage?

What should I do when my older children won't go to Mass?

How can I go to Mass if I have young children?

How can we keep our family together?

Leadership in the Church

Who is the pope to Catholics?

Is the pope infallible?

Does everything that the pope teaches carry the same weight of authority?

History has shown that popes haven't always been correct.

I read that a high percentage of Catholics don't follow the pope's teaching on birth control.

If popes made mistakes about the Inquisition, if Pope Alexander VI had illegitimate children, how can you put such faith in these sinful human leaders?

Despite all these papal failures, do you still want to hold onto the papacy?

Through the centuries millions of people have had a problem with the idea of the pope continuing the role of Peter. Why don't you join the reformers?

Why are there so many levels of membership in the Catholic Church: pope, bishops, monsignors, priests, deacons, and then, the bottom of the rung, the laity? Aren't we all called to be one in Christ?

I heard that some archbishop left the church with many of his followers. Would you tell me about that?

Why are priests called "Father"?

Recently I've heard about some Catholic priests going to jail for molesting children or getting girls pregnant. What's going on?

What should I do when hurt by a priest who
   spoke rudely to me?

Women

Women don't have much voice in church
   decisions, do they?

Why are Catholic leaders so opposed to women
   becoming priests?

Sacrament of the Sick

What is the special ritual that Catholics have for
   the dying?

What do Catholics believe about miracles?

Is it un-Christian to fear death?

Why do some Catholics have wakes?

SECTION 4
Catholic Moral Teaching 177

Sexual Morality

I see church leaders frequently acting out of
   frustrated sexual lives and trying to control the
   sexuality of others. Be married for twenty
   years. Raise five children and then talk to me
   about sexuality.

I get the impression that the church is
   preoccupied with saying no to sex, especially
   sexual intercourse.

Homosexuality

What do Catholics believe about homosexuality?

Should we use the mass media to encourage
   people to use condoms to save our nation from
   AIDS and unwanted pregnancies?

Isn't the scourge of AIDS a punishment from
   God?

Birth Control and Artificial Insemination

Why is the Catholic Church opposed to birth control?

What is the Catholic Church's stand on sperm insemination, embryo and sperm banks, surrogate parenthood, and test-tube-baby technology?

Why does the Catholic Church oppose test tube fertilization for couples who can't have children by natural means?

What do you think of the controversy over frozen embryos?

Why is pornography bad?

Is masturbation permitted?

Abortion

Where do you stand on abortion?

What if the act of intercourse is not of love but of rape or simple sexual gratification? Or what if the couple would make a bad world for their child?

Does the fifteen-year-old girl who has just found out that her boyfriend "got her pregnant" have any freedom?

Don't you hear me? I must have the freedom to choose what happens in my body!

I don't agree with abortion. But in certain circumstances, like incest or rape, a woman must have her freedom!

But why should the mother, the victim of injustice, have to bear the burden of a child because of abuse by a man?

Generally, I must tell you that I deeply resent your smug, insensitive, and chauvinistic attitude toward women and their struggle for justice, freedom, and self-respect.

Are you one of those "single-issue voters," who will vote for any candidate who is against abortion?

Issues That Foster Life

Why are Catholic bishops so opposed to the death penalty? Doesn't the Bible say it is all right?

What's wrong with euthanasia? If a person is so sick or old that he or she can no longer be useful in life, shouldn't he or she be able to choose death?

Why should a person have to suffer? If medical aid can't take away the pain, then a person should have the freedom to choose death.

Morality in the U.S.A.

Is the United States a Christian country?

What do you think concerns Jesus about our nation?

Should an American Catholic endorse sending military equipment to a Central American country like El Salvador?

Several Catholic leaders have come out in favor of "sanctuary" for illegal aliens. Please explain this.

Politics and the Church

What is liberation theology?

Is Communism the greatest evil in the world?

How can our nation trust other countries, especially the Communists?

Should a Christian run for political office?

Is there something wrong with a politician's being pro-choice?

What about Catholic politicians getting involved in the inevitable political compromises?

What about the separation of church and state?

The church's stand for pro-life legislation has an unfair influence on those who are not Catholic.

You say that you want to keep the separation of church and state. I don't believe it. A quick look at history shows that Catholic politicians, kings, priests, bishops, and popes have wielded great political power to foster Catholic interests. Do you want to get back into power?

Why is the Vatican a sovereign state? You want the best of two worlds, religious and secular.

SECTION 5
Catholics and People of Other Beliefs 221

Salvation

What do you believe about salvation?

Are you sure you are saved?

What is purgatory?

What is an indulgence?

Do Catholics believe that they're the only ones who will go to heaven?

Christian Unity

What is the meaning of the word *Catholic*?

I feel prejudice against people of other denominations and other religions.

Why are Catholics and protestants so cold to each other?

How do you justify the Inquisition?

Why don't Catholics permit non-Catholics to receive Communion at Mass?

Catholics and Non-Christian Religions

What do you think about the New Age Movement?

Why have Christians treated Jews so badly?

Why is it that people who believe in God— Christians, Jews, Hindus, and Muslims—seem to have problems getting along?

Are you contradicting Jesus' words that salvation comes only through Him?

To say all that means an end to the missionary mandate that was so clear in Jesus' teaching.

What are Catholics doing as foreign missionaries?

What about Catholic missionary work here in the United States? For instance, there seem to be very few Catholics in the black community.

So now you are going to get out there and start snatching up those black protestants to get them into the Catholic Church?

What about missionary work among the new immigrants; among the Hispanics?

What about Orientals?

Catholics have so much money! Why aren't they on television like the protestant fundamentalists?

Should we work for unity with people of non-Christian religions?

Can you give an example of people who are doing this?

SECTION 6
Conclusion 251

In the midst of pluralism and challenge, you have decided to remain Catholic. Can you explain?

Acknowledgments

This book began more than ten years ago, thanks to the work of Mr. Bruce Anderson, who brought together many of my answers in a little book I published myself. Since then I have written a weekly column in the *Los Angeles Herald Examiner.* I have been able to incorporate some of those columns into the present book. Talk radio programs have provided the questions. I have been enriched by conversations with my friend Dennis Preger on his radio program, "Religion on the Line," on Sunday nights on Los Angeles' KABC and, more recently, by working with the ever-challenging Carol Hemingway on her talk radio program.

I am pleased to thank Mattie McGivney and Barbie Webb, who offered their direction during the early stages of the writing. Then as the book progressed, I was able to use the insights of Janet Thoma, who is an acquisitions editor for Thomas Nelson Publishers. Janet's support and interest were the keys to getting this book into print. Donna Sherwood, from the faculty of the University of Tennessee, used her amazing talents to polish my grammar and style. Tom Shaw, another editor-friend from San Diego, gave me a critical look as to how I was coming across to Catholics.

Because I want to make sure that what I write is not contrary to the teaching of the Catholic

ACKNOWLEDGMENTS

Church, I submitted the book to my superior and close friend, Father Joseph Miller, SVD. He passed the book along to theologian Father Al Zimmerman, SVD, who made his thorough review from a hospital bed where he was recovering from hip surgery.

When I offer thanks, I want to give a special niche to my friend Jim Calvagna. Along with offering editorial input, he is responsible for nursing along my love affair with computers. I thank him for his availability, patience, and "smarts" when it comes to the machine that has made writing, and especially rewriting, a joy.

My final and deepest thanks go to Father Pat Connor, SVD. His humor, wisdom, honesty, talent, and love have been invaluable. He painstakingly worked through the manuscript with me. Thank you, Pat.

Introduction

The Jewish host on a radio program asked, "Do you believe that Christianity is the true religion?" Now that is a basic question, isn't it?

I answered, "Yes, Jesus is the Son of God, the revelation of the Father's love. Yes, Jesus is the key to everyone's salvation."

My response came from various corners of my life. I have investigated Jesus in my head. I have asked the important questions about Him. Did he actually live two thousand years ago? I have studied His life and teaching in Scripture to discover if He is divine. I have read the accounts of Christians from the first century to the present and tried to understand the fullness of what Jesus revealed. My conclusion? Jesus was a real person who lived on this earth, and He spoke the truth. He is God.

After I consulted my head, I went to my heart. Jesus is to me much more than a historically verifiable person. I have experienced Him in my life. He is a real person who loves me. I experience this love when I read the Bible, when I see a sunset, and when I am loved by my friends. I experience Jesus' love profoundly through His forgiveness of my many sins.

Is Jesus a private affair?

I sometimes wish that my love for Jesus could be a private affair. Often I would like to be a Christian who goes alone to some mountaintop and reads Scripture and other spiritual readings. In this secluded world, I could experience God in meditation on streams, clouds, and the stirrings in my heart. Sounds idyllic.

The problem with Jesus is that He says that to love Him properly, I must also love others. Ah, there's the rub! As I seek communion with and love of God in personal study and meditation, I must come down from the mountaintop and love the repulsive woman who smells bad and talks too much. I must find God in the AIDS patient and even in the person who hates me. Impossible task? Certainly seems so.

To help me in this difficult task, Jesus formed a *community* of followers. Jesus' plan wasn't just that we make a personal commitment to Him—although this is necessary. Integral to our commitment to Jesus is a commitment to the Christian community.

It is important that we belong to a church because in the struggle with and support of fellow Christians, we find Jesus. This community of fellow believers will help us to address the difficult task of loving others. These people will share our love for the Lord. They will understand our striving to live up to the challenge of Jesus by worshiping with us, laughing with us, crying with us, and sometimes giving us a swift kick in the pants when we go haywire. This collection of people is a gift from God.

A Divided Christian Community

Unfortunately, because of different interpretations of Jesus' teaching, there is a scandalous disunity among the various Christian communities. Sometimes the separation is overt and includes name-calling. Sometimes one group of Christians claims that another group is going to hell. Some Christians express their prejudice against other Christians in jokes and paternalistic isolation.

Many Christians seem indifferent to the diversity and say, "It doesn't matter what church you attend. Jesus is the truth. As long as you believe in Him, the church is secondary." Many of these people remain in the denomination in which they were raised without much critical reflection on the whys and wherefores of their denomination: "If it was good enough for mama, it is good enough for me."

Others become "church-hoppers." They don't feel rooted in any particular denomination. They never seem able to make a commitment to a particular community. For some this is a quest for truth. For others it is a quest for gratification.

Even if we want to be indifferent to the problem of disunity, our disinterest is repeatedly challenged. Thanks to airplanes, cars, radio, and television, we no longer can be unaffected by the beliefs of others. No member of a denomination or religion can remain untested by other beliefs and practices. Through media, we have Christians and non-Christians of all types talking to us in our living rooms. The people on our block, if we cared to ask, would be Christians, Muslims, Jews, Buddhists, and atheists.

Such external influence is often still manageable. We are good at setting up defenses against people who think differently from us. The real challenge to our indifference to others' beliefs comes when our family is affected. For example, you, a Pentecostal, find youself madly in love with a Catholic; or, your neat little Baptist family is shaken when your daughter comes home to announce she is going to marry a Methodist. Or perhaps the greatest challenge comes when your teenager asks you why your denomination has done something for generations and you can't convince him with your answer.

Faith Is a Challenge

My commitment to the Lord and to my church is a blessed gift. God is the source of my faith. But my faith must be continually exercised. A gift of faith is similar to a little orange tree some friends recently gave me. Like the tree, my faith must be planted, watered, trimmed, and protected to insure a good crop.

I must strive to understand my gift of faith. A commitment to God in a certain denomination or religious group is never without questions and challenges to make sure the commitment is real.

An examination in faith is not a negative, muckraking inquiry. There is a foundation of hope and love for the Lord and His church. But that doesn't mean that my examination will be without some hard looks at certain human traditions that have lost their meaning. I can even question what leaders of the Church say and do.

Such loving criticism is a hallmark of Christianity. Jesus took the lead. Although he had deep love for the Jewish religion, He called religious leaders hypocrites for putting human interpretations of the law before peoples' needs.

There are two ways of dealing with this examination of our church. We can work to change things from the inside. This is extremely painful and a test of patience. The second way is also painful. We can wash our hands of the problems we encounter in our church and start a new church. Because of the frequent recourse to the second way, we have today over twenty-four thousand denominations of Christians.

Christ's Call to All People

As we strive to reconcile our church's beliefs and practices with the revelation of Jesus, we must remember a great responsibility. With the same drive of Christ, we are called as His followers to bring all people to God.

In the Gospel of John Jesus prays that all may be one. That is an urgently important challenge to Christians today. If we are going to follow Jesus in His tireless drive to bring all people to His Father, then we Christians must get together.

Christians aim to call the world to Jesus. We Christians can't significantly express the word for God while we bicker with each other. As we Christians are discontent with one another, the non-Christians are saying, "Well, if Christians can't come together, why should I listen to them, much less join them?"

The key to overcoming the scandal of Christian disunity is twofold: prayer and dialogue.

Christians of various denominations must pray for and with each other on a regular basis. Without this first step, dialogue is impossible.

Dialogue is a form of communication that is frightening. Many of us prefer a *monologue*. "I've got something to say so you shut up and listen." The other communication is *dualologue*, two people saying exactly what they think without one hearing anything of what the other says. With *dialogue* there is a surrender. I stop listening only to myself and what I want to hear and start caring to understand other people and their beliefs.

The danger of dialogue is that I may have to change my comfortable world view of smug superiority. I may have to admit that another denomination has an aspect of the truth in a much more profound way than I have learned it. This fearful dialogue is the key to attaining the unity for which Jesus prays.

Prior to my getting involved in dialogue with people of other denominations, my religious milieu was exclusively Catholic. My mom and dad were dyed-in-the-wool Catholics. Several generations back, there was a great-great-grandfather who was Dutch Reformed from Holland, but he became Catholic when he fell in love and married a young Irish lass in Chicago.

For eight years I went to a Catholic grade school. During those years the Roman Catholic church offered no dialogue with people of other religions. Catholicism was the one true faith, and everybody else was wrong. Although I never heard the exact words taught, there was quiet realization that if you weren't Catholic, at least with some kind of desire, you wouldn't make heaven. As a youngster I found that disturbing since my best friend was Doug Nanninga, a Lutheran. He loved God as much as I did, if not more. And one of my favorite relatives was Uncle Elmer, a non-Catholic who didn't even go to church. Would all the love and care he gave to people go unrewarded?

My Catholic isolation became stonger as I went

to the seminary at age fourteen. Our intense study of the Bible and church teaching was never done in a flesh and blood dialogue with non-Catholics.

Then in the beginning of the sixties, a revolution happened in the Catholic Church. The pope, a roly-poly Italian by the name of John XXIII, called all the Catholic bishops of the world to Rome for a gutsy reevaluation of Catholicism. The main question I heard from the discussion of the bishops was, "How can the Catholic Church renew itself today to teach the revelation of Jesus better?"

In an unprecedented step, the pope invited protestant and orthodox observers to be part of the council. The pope called the observers "Brothers." A new dialogue was beginning. The window was flung open, and the surge of the wind of the Holy Spirit rushing through made closure seem impossible.

In the seminary we started having days of dialogue with protestants. We even played some basketball together. And then, wonder of wonders, we invited a local rabbi to teach us the Hebrew Bible.

I am happy to say that in the years since I left the seminary, the Lord placed me in deep dialogue with Christians who are not Catholic. More than twenty years ago I was bitten by the bug of using mass media to share my love for Jesus with others. I turned to protestants for their expertise in evangelizing others through media. The dialogue that ensued has been exhilarating and disturbing but has always drawn me closer to Jesus, whom we share in common. I am happy to say that the dialogue has strengthened my commitment to the Catholic Church.

Unity and Not Uniformity.

Unity can be a frightening prospect if it is equated with *uniformity*. The unity that I look to will not demand that we ignore cultural and denominational styles that have developed through time. Christians of different denominations must respect each other. We must acknowledge that the Holy Spirit was and is present among people who sincerely seek God's truth.

The Audience of This Book

The first step toward Christian unity is for each denomination to come to a deeper understanding of and commitment to their particular experience of the good news of Jesus. Then Christians need to look around at the beliefs and practices of other denominations.

And so I've written this book for Catholics. I hope my answers will clarify beliefs that they may never have questioned. I want my words to be their incentive to dig more deeply into what they believe. My wish is that through reading this book, Catholics will have more confidence in sharing their faith with others.

I hope you protestants, too, will read this book. Though you are a protestant, perhaps your spouse, a good friend, or a fellow worker is a Catholic. You can tell they're Catholic by the statue of Mary they have on the dashboard of their car or by the way they sweep their hand over their body in the sign of the cross before a meal.

I would like to teach you a little finesse in talking with Catholics. Many people of good will bluster into a Catholic's life and blurt out, "Are you saved?" or "Do you know Jesus?" Those are very disturbing questions for a Catholic, especially when they come from a complacent, seemingly smug protestant who oozes paternalism. His worn Bible has several notches on the side—notches to denote previous Catholics he "got saved." A Catholic's first reaction to questions like the above is to snap back with, "Who died and left you God?" The discussion is halted before it starts.

If you want to talk about religion with friends or relatives who are Catholic, you have to be understanding, patient, and, above all, deeply loving. I'm going to give you some understanding—you need to supply the patience and love.

As a Catholic, I believe that by being a good Catholic I can attain salvation. I hope that after reading this book, you will agree.

The Questions

The questions I respond to in this book have come from Catholics, protestants, Jews, atheists, and agnostics I have known through the years. The way they have asked has been sometimes nice; sometimes, angry; sometimes, down right nasty!

We will move into our discussion gently. I'll start with *questions we all share* no matter what our religious background: How do I know God's will? Why am I not happy? How can I overcome failure? And how can I trust others after I have been repeatedly let down by others?

A Catholic's *spirituality* frequently seems different from a protestant's on several key issues: Do Catholics read the Bible? Is love for Jesus lost with Catholics because of their involvement in ritual and tradition? What do Catholics do when they worship on Sundays? Are Mary and saints more important than Jesus? Do Catholics believe in exorcism? And how do Catholics reconcile a loving God with personal tragedies?

The *seven sacraments* are key moments in a Catholic's relationship with Jesus. Under the heading of these sacraments I will treat questions about infant baptism, the charismatic movement, confession of sins to a priest, the real presence of Christ in the Eucharist, annulments of marriages, why the Pope is so important to Catholics, and Catholics' beliefs in miracles and healing.

Catholics take strong *moral stands* on sexual matters. I will roll up my sleeves and field questions on abortion, birth control, homosexuality, masturbation, and pornography. Beyond sexuality, morality also involves concern with nuclear weapons buildup, the death penalty, guarding the lives of the elderly, and U.S. involvement in Central America.

The final part of the book will look at Catholics' *relationship with protestants and people in non-Christian religions.* Do Catholics believe these people are saved? What do Catholics think about unity with protestants? Can a Jew attain salvation without becoming a Christian?

Please listen with an awareness that I am honestly seeking the truth. I don't want to dodge any questions, not even the more difficult ones or the angry ones.

You can read this book straight through or simply look at the issues that are most interesting to you. You can also consult the index at the back of the book to find the topics you wish to read.

SECTION 1

The Struggles We Share

Being a Christian doesn't mean that I am free from personal problems. Life this side of heaven is filled with joy, peace, and love but also struggles, fears, frustrations, and failure. With St. Paul we can at one time say, "Yet I live, no longer I, but Christ lives in me" (Gal. 2:20). Most Christians can look back on their lives and remember that warm experience. But at other times we can more easily understand St. Paul when he said, "For I do not do the good I want, but I do the evil I do not want" (Rom. 7:19).

The first step to a healthy Christian life is to admit to ourselves and to others that we are struggling. The second step is to reach out to others for help.

How can I find God's will for me?

Discerning God's will is often difficult, but He has given us several means to do it. The first way is devout prayer, which includes listening. We often ask God in prayer to guide us, but we don't wait in silence for an answer! Another problem is that if we *do* listen, God's answer may be something we prefer not to hear.

Our prayer to find God's will should be combined with the reading of Scripture. Find a Bible that has a topic reference, and then read the various passages that pertain to your struggle.

Look to the example of good people you know or have read about. There are others, just like you, who have wrestled with the same dilemma.

Talk with people in your praying community. Seek their direction and their prayers.

Once you believe you have discerned God's will, move in that direction with conviction. You will know you are doing God's will when His signs of peace, love, and joy accompany your actions.

At other times you will not be completely confident that you should act one way or the other. Given such confusion, many people stagnate in indecision. Sometimes we have to act without the security of complete certitude. Throughout history God has called people to step out in faith in spite of questions and doubts.

Why am I not happy?

God wants me to be happy by relaxing in His power. But I have often responded by choosing anxiety or even despair rather than "letting go and letting God." I have preferred to deal with the tangible rather than with God's power.

I will be happy when I praise God with my mouth, study Him with my mind, and submit to His will in my everyday actions.

I will not be happy when I am concerned primarily with my own pleasure. Selfishness, pride, and my need to control other people don't really make me happy.

Happiness, according to God's plan, comes when I serve the needs of others with the same intensity that I care for my own desires. This is fine when it makes us feel good, as at Christmas. I am not too bad at loving people I love. But God stretches me when He asks me to love those I don't like, even those who are my enemies.

Is it a sin to feel inferior?

Feeling inferior is wrong when we use the feeling to excuse ourselves from not developing our God-given talents. As long as we say, "I can't do that because I feel inferior" or "I'm afraid to go there because I feel inferior," we don't have to grow into the fullness to which God has called us—that abundant life. We need to recognize the talents God has given us, then use them to give Him glory.

My own struggle with feeling inferior is frequently tied into the comparisons I make between myself and others. If I try to write a book, I can always find someone else who could do it better. If I take up racquet ball or playing the piano or try to start a business or learn a new language—the list is endless—I can always find someone who can do better.

Our national psyche is so imbued with the ideal of being number one that we don't risk beginnings because we fear we'll never be the best.

God has made each of us unique. Whatever we do will be special in and of itself. We can use comparisons to improve ourselves but not to hinder risking the use of our talents.

One of the most practical ways of overcoming a sense of inferiority is to reach out and build up those who have similar negative feelings. When we do this, wonderful things happen to improve our self-images.

My faith seems to be stagnating. How can I grow spiritually?

To grow spiritually, we need to think spiritually. That may involve reading the Bible frequently, listening to "Christian tapes," reading spiritual books, attending seminars, sharing our experiences of God with others, and spending time quietly listening to Him. In our fast-paced society, we often feel we should be doing something all the time, but God often calls us to be still and listen, allowing His power to change and mature us.

A danger in growing spiritually is that when we reach a comfortable stage in our relationship with the Lord, we decide to rest there. But the Lord is continually calling us to deepen our commitment to Him. Only through a strong commitment to Jesus will we be able to grow spiritually. Remember: whatever stagnates, dies.

How should I handle negative feelings?

Jesus never said, "I want you to *feel* good about God, your neighbor and yourself," but He did say that He wants us to *love* God, love our neighbors, as we love ourselves. Feelings are a vital part of life, but too often they get undue emphasis. We don't have to feel good about someone who lives on skid row, but we can still reach out to him, love him, and care for him.

We should love ourselves in the same way. We might be overwhelmed by our failures, but that shouldn't stop us from doing all we can to touch the magnificence of what God has given us. Each of us is a child of God, a temple of the Holy Spirit, a brother or sister of Jesus, made in the image of God, God's work of art.

Finally, even if we experience tragedy and feel God has rejected us, we shouldn't allow these feelings to make us believe we are unloved by God. We should accept feelings as part of being human, but not permit them to rule us or prevent us from doing what Jesus demands.

Why is patience important?

Patience furthers peace of mind and soul. If we are patient, we release from our shoulders an unnecessary burden of anxiety and control. To choose patience is to have wisdom.

My model for patience is the way God deals with me and my sins. Instead of coming down hard with punishment for my failings, God patiently urges me to change my ways.

Tests of patience can be found in (1) being patient with our weaknesses and failings; (2) being patient with others and understanding that they may be at different levels of development than we are; and (3) being patient with God, knowing that His plans are deeper and more secure than our fleeting wishes and desires. Good things come with patience.

Unfortunately, my prayer for patience goes something like this: "Lord, please, give me patience, but give it to me *now!*"

How can I keep from feeling discouraged?

The worst way to react to discouragement is to pretend that it isn't there, that it isn't bothering us. We need honestly to accept discouragement with all its attendant fear and heartache. Denial can turn discouragement into a big, ugly, longlasting monster.

For a Christian, the frailty of discouragement can be a doorway to greatness. Paul said, "I am content with weaknesses, insults, hardships, persecutions, and constraints, for the sake of Christ; for when I am weak, then I am strong" (2 Cor. 12:9). Also, the suffering and discouragement of the cross reminds us that Jesus has gone before us down the road of discouragement. We are not alone.

Discouragement usually shows that we are dependent on others. Facing this need and then reaching out to others for help can become the ingredients of excellence.

Besides meditation on these spiritual truths, we need to reach out in our discouragement to a friend who will listen to us and just be with us. Discouragement usually comes when we have experienced failure. We need to swallow our pride and honestly share our weakness with someone who will handle us with tenderness and understanding.

Soon after being ordained a priest I was assigned to teach high school religion in the Los Angeles ghetto of Watts. Despite initial enthusiasm for the assignment, I soon learned that I lacked the discipline skills to deal with teenagers in the classroom. After two years I had to leave the school. I had failed as a high school teacher.

The failure was devastating to me. I visited with my mom and dad, who lived near Los Angeles. One afternoon I shared with them my inability to handle the role of high school teacher. I remember their tender love and understanding.

I also turned to the Gospel of Mark. I found Jesus understood my failure. He knew failure in His dealings with His family, His disciples, the religious leaders, and the Gentiles. From reading of these discouraging experiences of Christ, I gained a strength to deal better with future struggles.

How can I recover from being hurt by a loved one?

My reactions to being hurt by a loved one can be feelings of disappointment or anger or frustration or confusion. But the overriding emotion is being unable to forgive. Once I can forgive the loved one, my disappointment, anger, frustration, and confusion become manageable.

One of the roads to forgiveness is understanding. I need to talk with the person who has hurt me to find out why the hurtful action was done. A good example of this happened when Mary questioned Jesus after she had lost Him for three days in the temple.

Remember that the ability to forgive someone who has hurt us deeply can be achieved only with the help of the Lord. At these times I simply cannot generate forgiveness on my own.

What if the person who has hurt me doesn't think his action requires forgiveness?

Then you need to talk to the other about your feelings so that the person knows where you are coming from. If he knows of the pain he has caused but is still not sorry, you should release yourself from feelings of guilt. You have done your part in seeking reconciliation. Pray that God will bless the person who has hurt you.

Remember that when God asks us to forgive others He doesn't assure us that we will feel good about the person who has hurt us. Despite negative feelings we must pray, speak and act in love toward the person who has hurt us.

Because my father was an alcoholic, I'm having problems as an adult. Should I just pray, or can I do something else?

By all means, pray. God's power is the key to the coming together of your life. When I was in a similar situation, God responded to my prayer in this way: two friends, quite independently of each other, introduced me to a fast-growing organization called Adult Children of Alcoholics. Both my friends had parents who were alcoholics.

When I mentioned that my mother and sister had a drinking problem and my sister died of cirrhosis of the liver, my friends treated me with all solicitude and lent me the latest books by psychologists working with the adult children of alcoholics.

I have found the reading material on ACA very helpful. And as I share in my sermons and talks some of the fears and obsessions that I have developed because of the alcoholic situation in my childhood, I find that significant numbers of Americans share my struggles.

Certain common characteristics are found in children brought up in households where there is an alcoholic or chemical dependency.

We have come to feel isolated, uneasy with other people, especially authority figures. To protect ourselves, we become people pleasers sometimes even losing our identity in the process.

We either become alcoholics ourselves or marry them or both. Failing that, we find another compulsive personality, such as a workaholic, to fulfill our sick need to be abandoned.

We have an overdeveloped sense of responsibility. We prefer to be concerned with others rather than ourselves. We somehow get guilt feelings when we stand up for ourselves rather than give in to others. Thus we become reactors rather than actors, letting others take the initiative.

We are dependent, terrified of the very abandonment we have sought out. We are willing to do almost anything to hold onto a relationship in order not to be abandoned emotionally. Yet we keep choosing insecure relationships because they match our childhood relationship with alcoholic parents.

We learned to suppress our feelings as children, and as adults we keep them buried, confusing love and pity, tending to love those we can rescue. Because of the prevalence of anger in our family of origin, we have a hard time expressing anger and dealing with it in others. Even more self-defeating, we become addicted to excitement in all our affairs, preferring constant upset to workable relationships.

The road to recovery is a spiritual road similar to that of the twelve recovery steps for Alcoholics Anonymous. If you find that I have struck a nerve or two, I hope that you will do further reading on the subject and then perhaps join a weekly support group.

Why is trust difficult for me?

Trust is necessary for us to get through life. We need to trust ourselves to reach for our dreams. We need to trust others to do the vitally important work of accepting our fragile, vulnerable selves. And we need others.

Trust is extremely difficult to hold onto. Perhaps because of personal failures in our past, we shy away from trusting ourselves. We know that nine times out of ten we are going to fall into a repetition of past sins. Because others have repeatedly failed us, we dread being foolish enough to trust others and so make ourselves vulnerable to hurt. We don't want to get burned again.

Unfortunately the result of this withdrawal is that we become isolated. Without the risk of trust, fear and misunderstanding of ourselves and others begin to rule our lives.

Does God answer all prayers?

Yes. He responds not only to our immediate problem, but also to our needs far into the future.

Be careful when you say God doesn't answer

your prayers. You are probably standing in the magnificence of His answer but have too small an expectation to see the all-embracing love with which He has responded.

Loving parents know that a child thinks they are unloving when they refuse to give more candy than the child needs. The child can't anticipate the pending stomach ache. Parents seem mean when they demand that their sick child make a trip to the doctor who sticks a long needle into the child's arm. Like the child, we can be more concerned with immediate gratification than with goodness and happiness in the long range.

How do I find time for proper prayer?

As you attempt to find prayer time, it's essential to ask yourself how important such quiet time is in your life. If Jesus were to come in the flesh, as he did two thousand years ago, would you have time for Him? His presence is just as strong a reality right now, and you should give priority to Him in your day.

Be careful, though: if you set up a scheduled time to pray, don't become rigidly locked into it. Set priorities, but be flexible if someone who is in immediate need steps into your life.

SECTION 2

Catholic Spirituality

How do you relate to God? Jesus has answered this question for us. Through His revelation, we know God. Thanks to this revelation, we know that God wants to communicate with us, and He wants us to respond.

In this chapter I will explain how Catholics understand this revelation of Jesus and respond in prayer and worship. Catholics understand Jesus' revelation being passed on to us by both the written word that we call the Bible and also the revelation that was passed on through word of mouth.

The Bible

Why don't Catholics stress reading the Bible more?

Regretfully, many Catholics like me were not raised with the love and appreciation for reading the Bible. In my own home we didn't read the Bible, and in grade school I had only a cursory exposure to the sacred Book. When I went to Mass, the Scriptures were read in Latin, and I followed along with a book that had an English translation.

In the 1940s Pope Pius XII opened the Bible to study by Catholic scholars in a new way. He asked them not always to interpret the Bible literally. He wanted them to ask some very basic questions as they read God's word: who wrote what, under what circumstances, when, where, and why? He thought that scientific inquiry into the cultural background of the Bible would help to plumb the depths of the Bible's true meaning.

This opened a floodgate of interest among Catholics in the study of the Bible. Twenty years later, when the Catholic bishops from all over the world met in Rome for what is called the Second Vatican Council, they put a new stress on individual reading of the Bible and group study.

With the Mass now in English, the readings for daily and Sunday Masses were organized so that over three-year cycles, Catholics could hear most of the Bible read at Mass. Priests were called on to preach each Sunday on the Scriptures and to offer at daily Mass a homily based on the Scripture readings.

When I was in the seminary, I studied the books of the Hebrew Bible and then read the New Testament many, many times. In my last years of seminary, I had four years of intense Bible study.

Today a Catholic parish that doesn't have a Bible study group is more and more an exception.

How did Catholic reluctance to read the Bible begin?

Prior to the Reformation, Catholics were not reluctant to read the Bible. The fact is that until the printing press was invented, education of the masses was at a very low level in comparison to today. Those Catholics who were educated were able to center their spirituality around the Bible. I am thinking of outstanding Scripture scholars like Origen, Jerome, and Augustine. Thomas Aquinas based his theology on a deep understanding of the Bible.

Until the printing press, education of the masses was at a very low level, by today's standards. Handwritten copies of the Bible were difficult to produce. Because these copies were so few and precious, they were often chained to the lectern in a church to make sure they were not stolen.

At this time, a style of Christian living arose in many places in the church that didn't seem to be in agreement with the Scripture: clericalism was rife; there were the money-making indulgences, avarice, papal military power; good works became more important than faith; and an impersonal ecclesiastical bureaucracy stifled the freedom of the Spirit.

The reformers revolted against all this and based their actions on various verses of the Bible. Once the Bible was translated into the vernacular and mass produced by the newly invented printing press, education of the masses improved, and people could read firsthand the arguments of Luther and the other reformers.

Christianity was divided into two camps: the protestant camp, those who thought the Bible was the sole authority in religious matters; and the Catholic camp, those who thought the pope together with tradition and Scripture was the sole authority. Catholics moved to the defensive. Catholic authorities greatly feared "private interpretations of the Bible." Although the Bible had been and was still the Word of God, the free reading and private interpretation of the Bible was kept in the hands of clerics. The laity were told to be cautious lest they misread the Bible as the reformers had done.

Fortunately, today, Catholics are encouraged to read and study the Bible.

Isn't the written Word all we need of God's revelation? Why do Catholics also need tradition?

The Catholic views the Bible as a vital source of revelation inspired by the Holy Spirit. The Bible is the way for us to learn of the revelation of the Father in Jesus and the Holy Spirit.

The revelation of the Father comes to us in two forms, both valid: the first came through word of mouth; and then the New Testament records some of that oral tradition. After Pentecost the apostles and disciples spread what Jesus had taught them among people living around the Mediterranean. Paul's letter to the Thessalonians is the earliest piece in the New Testament. Scholars date it around the year A.D. 50. We don't know of any written account of Jesus' life and teaching until Mark's Gospel, which was written around the year A.D. 70. The last Gospel, John's, probably wasn't written in its final form until about A.D. 90. If Jesus died around the year 30 that means that the transmission of His revelation depended on word of mouth to a great extent in the years after Jesus' death and resurrection.

Catholics believe that the Holy Spirit was with the Church during those times in both the spoken and written records of Christ's life and teaching.

We Catholics respect both the sacred tradition that is written and that which was passed on by word of mouth. John said at the end of his Gospel, "There are many other things that Jesus did, but if these were to be described individually, I don't think the whole world would contain the books that would be written" (John 21:25). St. Paul speaks of the oral and written tradition when he writes, "Therefore, brothers, stand firm and hold fast to the traditions that you were taught, either by an oral statement or by a letter of ours" (2 Thess. 2:15).

How do we assess those oral traditions that aren't explicitly found in the Scriptures?

We look to the beliefs and teachings in the early Church. Just as the Church needed to discern which of the many writings about Jesus were to be included in the final edition or canon of the Bible, so the church continues to clarify other beliefs of divine revelation. Catholics believe, for example, in Mary's lifelong virginity, her immaculate conception, and her assumption because they were facts of revelation known through a verified tradition, although they are not found in the written tradition of our Scripture. These sacred traditions never contradict the written word.

What do Catholics believe about tradition?

A Catholic who speaks of tradition distinguishes between sacred tradition and human tradition. God reveals sacred tradition, which will not change: For example, in the Trinity there are three persons in one God. On the other hand, human traditions can change: For example, the Mass was said in Latin for four hundred years and now is said in vernacular languages.

As a Catholic, I have never read the Bible. Can you make this book less intimidating to me?

God is a great talker. He has spoken to us at many times and in many places. Much of what He has said has been written down by those who love to listen to Him. What He's said has been put into a collection of books which, today, we call the Bible.

What kind of books are in this collection? Stories, poems, histories, songs, wise sayings, promises of love, prophecies, and advice on how to live and how to die.

Some sections you will not be able to stop reading because of the sheer excitement the stories engender. You will meet all kinds of people: heroes, villains, saints, sinners, cowards, beauties, and hags. You will find the clever and the stupid, the powerful and the weak. You will read about the devil himself. But most of all you will come to know and love the Father and His beloved Son, our Lord Jesus Christ, and the Holy Spirit.

When were the books written? The first books appeared about 900 B.C., and the last one was written around A.D 100.

Why were they written? Because God wanted to express in writing how much He loves us.

Where should a Catholic start reading the Bible?

I would begin by reading the Acts of the Apostles. This is the story of the early church after Jesus had ascended to heaven. It is an exciting book, filled with many experiences similar to those that you go through in your own life.

Next, I would suggest that you go to the first Gospel account that was written: the good news of Jesus according to Mark. This shortest of the Gospels gives an image of Jesus that we can easily relate to. Here we see His humanity, His love, His anger, His frustrations, and His burning spirit.

Then move on to God's loving power at work among the patriarchs—Abraham, Isaac, Jacob, and Joseph, who are found in the book of Genesis. Marvel at the Lord's continuing plan of salvation as He touches the stuttering and shy old man, Moses, and calls him to lead His people out of

Egypt into the promised land. You'll find this account in the book called Exodus.

Observe God's care for David in the Book of Kings. Read on from the young boy's familiar battle with Goliath, to his struggles to become king, to his unfaithfulness with Bathsheba, and even to the attempt on his life by his son Absalom. God loved this man David mightily and gave him rich blessings despite His many sins and failings.

One of the most passionate accounts of the Lord's love for us is found in a book called "the Song of Songs." The Lord uses the longing and desire of a lover for His beloved to convey the intensity of His love for us.

Finally go back to the very beginning of the first book of the Bible, Genesis. End this introductory walk through the Bible with the story of God's loving plan of creation for us.

The Bible is a living book. It is the Lord really speaking to us every time we read it.

I know that the average person has many apprehensions about picking up the Bible. It often seems shrouded in mystery. Perhaps there is even a fear that reading the Bible will cause problems for one's faith rather than blessings.

Well, to give in to these feelings is to miss one of the most enlivening encounters with God that you can ever have.

Remember as you read that you are not merely recalling people and events that happened many years ago. The Bible transcends time. It is the story of how God loves you right now.

What's the difference between the Catholic and Protestant Bibles?

Catholics and Protestants share the same New Testament. For a while Luther considered Hebrews, James, Jude, and Revelation as inferior and put them at the end of his New Testament translation. Calvin seems to have had reservation about 2 and 3 John. Eventually all differences were reconciled and protestants and Catholics agreed with the fourth-century church councils, which established the approved listing of books of the New Testament as we have them today.

The Catholic version of the Hebrew Bible differs from the protestants'. The Catholics have a Greek version called the Septuagint, which was used by Hellenistic Jews in Alexandria in North Africa. Luther chose a Hebrew version, which was used by Jews in Palestine. The protestant version does not include the books of Tobit, Judith, Wisdom, Sirach (Ecclesiasticus), Baruch, 1 and 2 Maccabees, and that part of Daniel called the book of Susannah.

The Septuagint or Catholic version was used by most of the writers of the New Testament when they wanted to quote from the first writings of the Bible. Also all of the Septuagint books, except for Esther, are found in the recently discovered Dead Sea Scrolls.

Why is the Catholic Church against a literal interpretation of Scripture?

The Bible is the Word of God, inspired by the Holy Spirit. If we always take it literally we cramp the style and power of what God is saying.

For example, when Jesus says in Luke 14, "If anyone comes to me without hating his father and mother, wife and children, brothers and sisters, and even his own life, he cannot be my disciple." Some people have taken these words literally and have harshly cut themselves off from people who love them and to whom they owe some responsibility. Although God challenges us, He also asks that we act with the wisdom of common sense and balance.

Interestingly, Catholics at times adopt a more literal interpretation of the Scriptures than some fundamentalists. This can be seen in a greater stress on the real presence of Christ in the Eucharist, which a Catholic understands from Christ's words, "This is My body" (Mark 14:22).

Would you encourage a Catholic who wants to go to a nondenominational Bible study?

That's like asking if you can send your child to any college he chooses. It all depends on who the teachers are and what they are teaching.

If you are a Catholic, I advise you to be discreet in choosing a Bible class. Remember that there can be differences in understanding the revelation of Jesus. You might find a non-Catholic teacher who plays down the importance of Peter as the head of the apostles or for whom the Eucharist might only be a symbol or who says Mary might have had children other than Jesus or that Jesus might not be seen as equal with the Father and Holy Spirit. Even the best intended nondenominational Bible study groups can hold beliefs contrary to Catholic teaching.

If you don't have a good grasp on why you are a Catholic, perhaps you'll begin to doubt some of the teachings of the Church.

Before you begin Bible study in a nondenominational group, make sure you are well founded in the Catholic faith or have access to persons who can give you the Catholic interpretation of the Bible.

Jesus

Do Catholics "know" Jesus?

To know Jesus is a process similar to knowing your husband or wife, child, or friend. The question "Do you know Jesus?" can imply a plateau where you know all. That's unrealistic. You never know a person fully. Knowledge of a person is an unending quest.

An infant knows his or her mother; a child knows a friend; a teenager knows the girl he feels undying love for; newlyweds profess deep knowledge of each other; a couple celebrating fifty years of marriage say they know each other. Each of these people does know the other person, yet in an incomplete way. Experience and time allow relationships to grow deeper.

So it is with our knowledge of Jesus. Yes, we may know Him and experience Him at one stage in our lives, but we must always be open to a more profound knowledge.

Certainly, Catholics know Jesus. The challenge is to know Him more and more.

Be careful when you quiz people about their knowledge of Jesus. I have learned to be nonjudgmental when I evaluate another person's relationship with God.

How do you personally respond to the question, "Do you know Jesus?"

I am peeved. Initially I become very defensive and want to prove how I have totally surrendered myself to Jesus through my prayer life, my daily celebration of the Lord's Word and Sacrament at the Eucharist, my vows of poverty, celibacy, and obedience, and. . . . Then I relax and thank the Lord that I'm ultimately answerable to Him and to no human being.

For me, and I believe most Catholics, the question, "Do you know Jesus?" is usually painfully arrogant and alienating.

Do Catholics believe that Jesus is God and man?

Catholics believe that Jesus is both God and man. The challenge of this belief is to strike a balance between the two.

At time, too much stress on His being God clouds His full humanity. When this happens, I have to struggle to understand His going through things I can relate to as a human. I have a hard time seeing Jesus as tired, excited, angry, sad, and even tempted.

This pulling back from Jesus' complete humanity is wrong. Jesus, who is God, became a human being to assure me, today, that He knows and loves me in all I am going through. He became human as a way of saying He loves me completely. To say less is to cheat Him of all He went through.

Holy Week is a time when I recall how completely Jesus faced one of my greatest concerns—my death. Jesus faces the fact that His life on this earth is going to end. Christ met death in all its terror and isolation, as no other human being had or would in the future. I say this because I think that Christ loved life more than any person.

One has only to glance through the Scriptures to feel the love Jesus had for nature. His teachings are filled with affection for God's creation: mountains, flowers, wheat, water, trees, lambs, and birds.

Yet more than nature and animals, Jesus loved people. Oh, did He love people! We see that love especially in His exhaustive, tender concern for the lame, the blind, and those afflicted with a disease like AIDS, the leprosy of our time. With what delicate compassion He reached out to sinners!

Nor was Jesus a loner. He traveled constantly with twelve apostles. A group of women were continually with Him as He went from town to town calling people to love His Father. He delighted in listening to people. He seemed to love to debate.

I don't believe the world has even known a person who loved the world and its people the way Jesus did. This overpowering love made Him dread death.

Just before His arrest, Scripture says that Jesus pleaded three times with His Father to allow Him to go on living. Perhaps He asked for another year of life. Perhaps He asked if He could go to Greece or Rome and bring about the world's salvation in some other way than that ugly death on the cross. The letter to the Hebrews says that Jesus "offered prayers and supplications with loud cries and tears to the one who was able to save him from death" (Heb. 5:7). I know Jesus felt my fear of losing the world I love and the people in it.

Yes, Jesus was human, but he was also God. Not

only is He one with me in my humanity, He raises me to new levels of hope and love when I accept his divinity. The Son of God has become one with me, not only in compassion but in the power that helps me to overcome the most discouraging problem. Jesus is God and man!

The story of Jesus doesn't end on Good Friday. On Easter Sunday He conquered death. He came to life. And this new life said "yes" to the physical world that I know and love. His body could be embraced. He could eat a hearty meal.

In believing in Christ's victory as the Son of God, my faith gives me the assurance that I too will live beyond my own death. More than that, my new life will not be some abstract floating on clouds while playing a harp! As Jesus appeared to His followers, my eternity will be lived with this body of mine. My body will be made new. Gone will be all my aches and pains. And the people I love on this earth? Yes, they will be with me in my transformed life. Oh, and the world I love will be with me: my plum tree, the birds, the sunsets, the crash of the waves, and the cooling breeze.

I know that in the risen Christ I have overcome death.

Why do Catholics talk about doctrine so much? Why not just talk about Jesus?

I have found myself thinking this way when I am with protestant brothers and sisters. "Jesus is the source of all unity," they say. "Let's keep our eyes on Him and not worry about doctrine."

Then I started to think about how inaccurate this line of thinking is. Most doctrines are centered on Jesus; they clarify the reality of the revelation we experience in Jesus. It's hard to ignore vital doctrines of faith such as that Jesus is divine and human or the resurrection.

Doctrines usually arise out of a need to clarify the difference between true and false revelation. Without the stability of doctrine, revelation can become unclear.

Doctrine becomes evil when it is a source of division in the church, used by insecure people to prove that one denomination is better than another. Doctrine should be a way to come to a greater understanding of the revelation of Jesus—not a means of division.

Jesus often criticized the Pharisees for their legalism, yet you Catholics seem to have laws for just about everything, don't you?

The laws of the Catholic Church are in a book called, *The Code of Canon Law.* Their purpose is to keep good order in the church and ensure the true freedom of Catholics. Let me quote Pope John Paul II in his introduction to the revised Code that came out in 1983:

> What is the Code? For an accurate answer to this question, it is necessary to remind ourselves of that distant heritage of law contained in the books of the Hebrew Bible and New Testament. It is from this, as from its first source, that the whole juridical and legislative tradition of the Church derives.
>
> For Christ the Lord in no way abolished the bountiful heritage of the law and the prophets

which grew little by little from the history and experience of the People of God in the Old Testament. Rather he fulfilled it (Matt. 5:17), so that it could, in a new and more sublime way, lead to the heritage of the New Testament. Accordingly, St. Paul, in expounding the mystery of salvation, teaches that justification is not obtained through the works of the law but through faith (Rom. 3:28; Gal. 2:16), nonetheless he does not exclude the binding force of the Ten Commandments (Rom. 13:8–10; Gal. 5:13–25, 6:2), nor does he deny the importance of discipline in the Church (1 Cor. 5 and 6). Thus the writings of the New Testament allow us to perceive more clearly the great importance of this discipline and to understand better the bonds which link it ever more closely with the salvific character of the Gospel message.

Granted this, it is sufficiently clear that the purpose of the Code is not in any way to replace faith, grace, charism, and above all charity in the life of the Church or of Christ's faithful.

Laws in themselves are not bad. They are a source of order for communities. The observance of good laws leads to freedom. For example, if I observe the law of stopping my car at a red light and move ahead when the light turns green, I am free to get where I am going. If I disregard the law, I run a good chance of being hit by another car. My freedom will be restricted by having to go to the hospital or jail or the grave. Laws become bad when they become more important than the people they serve. Christ opposed the Pharisees' corruption of the law, which meant that law didn't free, but enslaved people.

Worship

What is the "Mass" that Catholics go to on Sundays?

When the Mass was in Latin, the last thing the priest would say was, "Ite, Missa est" ("Go, you are sent . . .") The word "Mass" is a derivation of the Latin "Missa."

The Mass is also called "the Eucharistic celebration." The word *Eucharist* is derived from an ancient Greek word used by early Christians to describe the commemoration of the Lord's Last Supper.

Were you to attend a Catholic Eucharistic celebration, you would find much music blended with words of adoration, contrition, thanksgiving, and petition.

There are two main parts of a Eucharistic celebration. The first is the celebration of God's Word—usually three Scripture readings and a reflection on them by the priest. In the second part we do what Christ asked us to do in His memory at the Last Supper. We offer God the Father bread and wine and ask that they become the Body and Blood of Christ. The celebration ends with the reception of Communion by those present.

What is this sign of the cross that Catholics make over themselves?

Nothing complicated about it. The right hand passes from the head to the heart, to the left and then the right shoulder. Since the cross is the sign of our salvation, Catholics acknowledge that the crucified Savior is Lord of their lives when they trace it over their bodies.

As we make the sign of the cross, we ask that Christ renew the blessing of the cross in our lives. A Catholic who makes the sign of the cross in public is making a statement to others that he or she is committed to Christ.

At the door of every Catholic Church there is a little container of "holy water." It is called holy because it has been blessed, to remind us of the powerful water of baptism. A Catholic will touch this water and then trace the sign of the cross over his body and thus, however briefly, renew his baptismal commitment.

Is it okay for a Catholic to go to a different parish or denomination that suits her better?

There is a struggle in remaining faithful and loving in a parish of seemingly not excited Christians. Be cautious about leaving a parish or your own denomination because you have found another parish or denomination more to your spiritual and/or social liking. When we see people who are not as dedicated to Jesus as we think they should be, Jesus might be calling us to love them more. Our love can free them to accept Him more readily and with greater excitement.

We are called to change the world—including our parish—through a union with Jesus in long-suffering and patience. Strive to build up your spiritual leaders and fellow parishioners by affirming their positive qualities, thus freeing them to grow.

We will always find parishes and leaders who are not to our liking, but we must learn to keep our eyes on Jesus and the goal He has set for us through His church. The reality of Jesus Christ is in your parish; don't ignore it. People with whom we have difficulty can be a gift from God, leading us to a greater knowledge of ourselves and a heightened awareness of how much others need us. When we are in a tough position, He will give us the grace and strength to overcome obstacles that seem impossible.

So much for the ideal. Now get realistic. What happens when, no matter how hard you try, over a long period of time you find nothing but antagonism or a lack of spiritual nourishment?

I would not want to close the door on a person's freedom to choose another parish or to do what is necessary for spiritual nourishment.

If a person's peace of mind is at stake; if tension in a parish is causing physical illness; if the sermons are shallow and spiritual nourishment is nonexistent, I encourage Catholics to try another parish. This is easier in a large town where one can choose more easily.

Catholicism offers a great deal of diversity from one parish to another. A change of parish could offer one a fresh and more challenging approach to Jesus.

How can I change my "dead" parish?

There are several keys to bringing about effective change in a parish. The first is prayer and fasting. At the same time, a person should consult Scripture and a spiritual director in order to discern what positive steps might be taken to enliven a parish. The next step is to consult with others in the parish and share your views and concerns. Then together you should pray and fast to clarify further just what should be done.

After this, you should go to your minister or priest and share your concerns. When you speak to the minister or priest, be careful that you do not intimidate him or cause him to become defensive. People work better when they are not intimidated. Make sure that you convey your deep love, concern, trust, and willingness to listen. Don't assume you have all the answers; listen to the wisdom and insight your pastor has gained. After the conversation he will see the parish in a broader perspective.

Don't seek change for its own sake. When it comes to God and how to relate to Him, most people are very reluctant to change. They have worked things out to the extent that God is on their side. So woe betide the person who wants to go against what God and they think is best.

Be willing to work through the structures in the parish, like the parish council or the liturgical planning committee, even if they are part of the stifling influence. This might mean toning down some of your enthusiasm. Compromise is not a nasty word for two people who differ when pursuing the common good. As Thomas Aquinas said: "In living together, if everyone insists on his rights, you will have chaos." But be strong in your convictions and don't back down from healthy confrontation. Learn the art of loving confrontation. And it *is* an art!

It is important for Catholics in this situation to attend Mass frequently. Meet with members of the parish prayer group, under the direction of the pastor, to seek direction on how to allow the Holy Spirit to move in your parish.

What would a Catholic find if he/she decided to come back to church after many years away? Wouldn't he/she be uncomfortable?

A friend of mine came back to the Catholic Church in a way that made the transition less difficult. She began by attending a crowded Sunday Mass. She sat in the middle of the crowd so that she could tell from what others did when to stand and when to sit. On succeeding Sundays, she observed the priests in the parish say Mass. When she identified one she felt might be sensitive and understanding, she made an appointment and came in for the sacrament of reconciliation.

After celebrating the sacrament, she picked a parish activity that appealed to her. In my friend's case, she attended the weekly prayer group and Bible study group.

Another way of coming back is through a program called "The Rite of Christian Initiation for Adults" commonly referred to by the initials R.C.I.A. This is a program for those who want to become members of the church for the first time and for those who return after an absence from the church of many years. It is an ancient way to be instructed in and experience the life of the Church. An R.C.I.A. group meets at least once a week for discussion, learning, and to experience Catholic worship. One can be in the group for from six months to a couple of years. The program offers a time for an individual to discern whether to commit to Jesus in the Catholic Church. The program is closely related to the scriptural readings of each Sunday. A person usually completes the program and is received into the church on Easter.

I suppose there are other ways of coming back. You might break the ice with the support of a good friend or a relative. However you do it, know you are welcome!

Why do so many Catholics not go to church?

Of the 54 million Catholics in the United States, 40 to 50 percent do not go to church on a regular basis, according to studies by the Gallup Poll and the National Research Center.

What is wrong? The answers are many:

"I enjoy sleeping in on Sunday morning."

"I find my parish impersonal."

"The people in my parish are too conservative/liberal."

"Since they threw out the statues and started praying in English, I don't feel at home."

"I don't go to church to hug and shake hands with strangers."

"I have enough involvements in things in my life now. I don't need more involvements, not even in a church."

"Catholic priests never were able to preach."

"To be honest, the requirements of Christ are a bit more than I can handle."

"When the church starts acknowledging the equality of women with men, I'll come back."

"I disagree with the church's stand on birth control."

"The church's stand against abortion is sexist and insensitive."

"The bishops are too concerned about economics,

politics, and the military. They should confine themselves to spiritual matters."

"In the Catholic Church there is more concern with tradition than with a personal commitment to Jesus."

Despite all this negative reaction to the church, a person raised Catholic has a hard time disassociating completely from the church. The sociologist Father Andrew Greeley says, "In 1963, before the effects of the Second Vatican Council, 9 percent of those who were raised Catholics no longer identified with the church. By 1970, in the wake of the birth-control encyclical, the proportion had risen to 12 percent, and there it has remained ever since. Such a small increase in attrition—despite the highs and the lows, the ups and downs of the past twenty years—is remarkable."

I find those figures heartening. I had thought the percentages of those who had left the church were much higher.

Some research indicates that a high percentage of Catholics who drifted away between the ages of thirty and fifty are coming back. This might be attributed to a natural facing of adult responsibilities that give a new perspective to the value of the church.

Those in the thirty-to-fifty age bracket also face the sober reality of aging and death. The church offers concrete solace in the face of these realities.

Despite the church's weaknesses, it offers the person raised Catholic an ability to be in touch with the mystery of life, with community, and with sacramentality.

Catholics need to reach out actively to the large numbers of inactive Catholics. We need to respond lovingly to the complaints and objections of inactive members. On certain questions, a strong prophetic stand must be taken: no abortion, preference for the poor, opposition to war, and the proper expression of sex. But those objections that convict the church of impersonal legalism, judgmentalism, insensitivity, selfishness, and sloppiness in liturgy need to be listened to with caring and vulnerable ears. After we listen, we practicing Catholics must be willing to change to make the church more a place to come home to.

I don't go to church because I don't want to be a hypocrite. I'm not going to pretend I'm a saint like all those "holier-than-thou" people.

I understand a hypocrite to be a person who says one thing while his actions say something else. A hypocrite tries to impress others with a pretense of being good. People who go to church are often considered hypocrites by those who don't go.

When I helped out the Catholic chaplain at the state prison for women in California, the chaplain told me that the excuse used by many of the prisoners for not coming to the Catholic Mass was: "I might be a sinner, but I still have some vestige of integrity. I'm not going to pretend that I'm some kind of a saint by going to church." Although the prisoners' reasoning would seem to be quite commendable, they missed the whole point of going to church.

The reason that I go to church is that I'm not a saint. In fact, I know that I am very far from that goal. I go to church because I know I am a sinner, and I need the support and forgiveness of God and my fellow churchgoers to help me overcome my sins.

When churchgoers convey the impression that they are holier than those who don't go to church, they are wrong. The church is the home of sinners.

We must remember that Jesus' ministry was to those who were sinners: "Those who are well do not need a physician, but the sick do. I did not come to call the righteous but sinners" (Mark 2:17). The Bible is the story of many people like King David who sinned and were forgiven. If there were no sinners in church, no one would be in church. The more I go to church and come to know the Lord and how much He loves me, the more I become convinced that I am further from my goal of holiness.

That's why I love to celebrate Mass with prison inmates. Those who come to worship show much courage by going against the accusations that they are trying to be better than others. These prisoners I meet in church have an honesty, a vulnerability, and a need that makes the message of Jesus alive. They let down the mask of pretense. They know, better than most, how dependent they are on the Lord. Jesus is palpably present among prisoners who are strong enough to come to church.

Sometimes I wonder if most Catholics are just nominal Christians.

I must confess, I share your concern. I wonder why the almost one-fourth of our nation that is committed to Catholic values, doesn't have a more dynamic, positive impact on our country.

I've heard some say, "Catholics aren't any different from anyone else." Someone recently remarked to me, "I worked with a man for fourteen years, and I never knew he was a Catholic."

That's a shame. Being Catholic should make a person shine out unmistakably to the rest of the world.

But rather than point the finger at others, I must look at my own life. Why is it that being a Catholic doesn't make me feel any different from anyone else?

Sure, I love Jesus. He and His teachings are special in my life, but I'm often reluctant to let that be known to other people. I see people doing things that I know are unchristian, such as saying malicious things about others behind their backs or making ugly jokes about minorities. I don't have the nerve to stand up and say that gossip and racial jokes are not in line with my commitment to Jesus. Sometimes I even make things worse by joining in the backbiting and by laughing at racist jokes.

If you are anything like me, you dislike mediocrity. I like a person who is full of fire about his or her convictions and will make the truth known even in the teeth of anger, persecution, and the threat of bodily harm.

That's why the examples of outstanding Catholics are important to me. I need people like Pope John Paul and Mother Teresa. I need to recall the lives of past saints who went through the same struggles that I do and conquered. I need people who are just like me but who have stood up for the Lord and His teaching in most difficult situations.

How can we make sure that our lives as Catholics imitate the lives of outstanding examples of our faith? The foundation of being a Catholic responding fully to the call of Christ is found in certain basic actions: receiving God's assistance through the Eucharist, regular reception of the Sacrament of Reconciliation, frequent renewal of our baptismal vows in a true spirit of commitment, reading, and quiet meditation on the Scriptures.

If we are faithful in these ordinary things, we will be able to move beyond mediocrity. We will be able to bring the kingdom of the Lord to our families, our churches, our communities, our nation, and our world.

When we are confirmed as Catholics, the Holy Spirit brings a fire in our hearts that doesn't allow us to live our faith by the standard of "How far can I go before God gets mad?"

The Holy Spirit calls us to greatness and to be a sign of contradiction to the world.

Catholics seem to be proud of having so many members. Is it a blessing to be part of such a large and often impersonal organization?

One of the most serious difficulties of the Catholic Church in the United States is its large membership. There are some 54 million Catholics in our country. Although this certainly is a blessing, it also can create an obstacle to developing personal friendships in the church community. In many big-city parishes there are five to eight Masses on a weekend. The chances of a person sitting next to the same people on two successive Sundays are very small.

The Catholic Church can be very cold and impersonal. The goal of any church leader is to overcome this difficulty. One way is to help form small mutual-interest groups so that the members can come closer to the Lord through dialogue and interaction. Several small groups within the church can foster interaction while remaining part of the large church.

Cursillo is a good example. The word *cursillo* is Spanish for little course. A priest in Spain started this movement because he wanted to teach men and women in his parish some of the basics of the faith. A Cursillo involves four days of intense prayer, teaching, and fellowship. Strong bonds are formed among the members. These groups are encouraged to come together for prayer and study on a regular basis after the Cursillo weekend.

Through the years when my friends urged me to make a Cursillo, I always found other things to do. But eventually I "made my weekend." I was delighted. The fellowship was warm. The teaching was solid and based on personal experience.

Marriage Encounter is another movement that arose in the church to strengthen healthy marriages. Married couples who had been married for several years came together to renew their love and commitment. Through the guidance of other couples, new dialogue between spouses began. The result was a strengthening of marriages.

I made a Marriage Encounter. Granted I don't have a wife, I dialogued with another priest. We reevaluated our commitment to our community of fellow priests in a positive way.

Engaged Encounter is an offshoot of Marriage Encounter. With the rising number of divorces, the church sought a way to help a couple prepare for marriage by exploring the strengths and weaknesses of the relationship. Dialogue, the tool of Marriage Encounter, is used to open the channels of communication between the engaged pair.

The list of such small groups in the Catholic Church is long: the Vincent de Paul Society, charismatic prayer groups, Bible study groups, Knights of Columbus, and many others. I always encourage Catholics to join these groups to find close Christian community.

Why can't Mass be said in Latin?

The Latin Mass brought a sense of mystery to the celebration of the Eucharist. The Mass still is said in Latin in some churches. I believe, though, that the English Mass is popular because more people can understand it.

Is our society losing touch with the sacred?

I also wonder sometimes if anything is sacred any more. The abuse of drugs, alcohol, sex, and food is a sign to me that we are losing sight of the sacredness of the human body. In a selfish lust for pleasure, the addicts desecrate the temple of God and ruin the peace of those with whom they live.

To halt our rush for pleasure we should take stock of the place of the sacred in our lives. When I look for the sacred in my life, I think of special things that remind me of love and caring: the picture of my departed mother on my bureau, my dad's worn and cracked ring, and black-and-white family pictures.

Beyond these humanly sacred things, one of the keys to bringing back the sacred in our lives is a simple formula that the Lord gave us: "Keep holy the Lord's day." Attention to this commandment is pivotal to the reawakening of the sacred in our lives, individually and socially.

I am saddened to see the way shopping is often carried on to an even more intense degree on Sundays than on other days of the week. I wish that we would not encourage merchants on those days. I have started out my own little crusade. I refuse to buy things in grocery stores or shopping malls on Sundays. I wish that more people would join me in this so that the atmosphere on Sundays could be more conducive to rest, reflection, and recreation.

Recently I was in Israel at the time of Yom Kippur. I was amazed to see life in the Jewish area of Jerusalem come to a screeching halt. I was able to walk down the middle of normally busy streets. Every few blocks I heard Hebrew chants of worship coming from local synagogues. That experience called me to a greater need to make the Lord's day holy in my life.

Yet I think there should be a sense of balance in our observance of the Lord's day. Although I'm opposed to shopping, I do go to restaurants, service stations, and sporting events. Granted these activities do mean that some people will have to work on Sunday, but the work is more of a service to others in the cause of relaxation and recreation for others.

There is more to observing the Lord's day than going to church for an hour and then not buying and selling as one would on any other day. There's even more than watching football games and catching up on sleep. The Lord's day should also be a time in which we turn aside from our active world for a while—ten minutes, an hour—and quietly reflect on our relationship with Him. That can mean anything from watching a tree sway in the wind to meditating on a paragraph from Scripture. When we take this personal initiative to let God speak to us, we get in touch with the meaning of the sacred. Empowered by this new relationship with the Lord, we find ways to elevate our holy world to a new sacredness.

If Saturday is the Lord's day, why do Catholics worship on Sunday?

There was a struggle in the early church as to how to underline the difference between an Orthodox Jew and a Christian. Christians began to observe Sunday as the Lord's day because it is the day on which Jesus rose from the dead.

This practice of worshiping on Sunday does not mean observing Saturday as the Sabbath is wrong. But we Christians believe that a new order, a new creation, has come about through Jesus.

Why do priests wear elaborate vestments in church when Jesus wore such simple clothes?

Vestments are an attempt on our part to be in touch with a sacredness beyond our wildest imagining. They take on a new meaning in the context of Jesus' transfiguration. Jesus, in humble human form, was suddenly transformed in the midst of a world that was ready to crucify Him and bring him down; the apostles saw Him in His glory and power. When we wear vestments and clothes of celebration we are in touch with the Christ who lifts our hope to things above.

There are a variety of colors in the vestments. Each color has a significance:

- White or gold is for major celebrations like Easter and Christmas.
- Purple is worn in times of penance during Advent and Lent.
- Red recalls the blood of martyrs and the fire of the Holy Spirit.
- Green is the symbol of growth and is worn on most Sundays of the year.

The style of the vestments at Mass reminds us of our oneness with those who have worshiped God down the centuries.

A beautiful church, a chalice, and fine vestments serve to remind us that when we celebrate sacraments we are actually in the presence of the Godhead. Although we don't always dress and act in this solemn and mysterious way (any more than the transfiguration was a continual experience), we still need to try periodically to approach with awe God's transcending power through churches, sacred vessels, vestments, and rituals.

Why do Catholic churches have statues? Scripture is clear about "no graven images."

Statues of saints and even of the Lord are bad when they become more important than loving God and our neighbors. There were periods in church history when the importance of statues and pictures were overemphasized. Wood and plaster figures became objects of exaggerated, unhealthy veneration. There might have even been a tinge of idolatry attached. When this unhealthy attitude develops, the statutes and pictures should be taken away.

In addition, I am personally repelled by pictures

or statues of Jesus that make Him look anemic. I find this an insult to Jesus, who came to earth as a human being who was surging with feeling and who had His strength, courage, and tenderness in balance.

Just because some people act toward pictures and statues in an obsessive, unhealthy way, the use of pictures and statues as such should not be condemned.

For most Catholics, pictures and statues of Jesus and the saints are a healthy reminder of God's presence in our lives. They are reverend because of the person they represent, as we revere family pictures we display prominently in our homes. Such recalling of special people is wholesome and healthy and not the idolatry that the Lord condemns.

Do Catholics believe in fasting?

Catholics believe in fasting, for to go without food helps us to focus on the really important matters in a fast-paced and distracting world. Self-imposed fasting helps us to achieve discipline and a sense of sacrifice in what could be a self-indulgent life.

Fasting is also a way of praying. Fasting is pleasing to God and should often accompany the prayer requests we make to Him. Fasting says to ourselves and to the Lord, "I am serious about this petition." When we meet problems that seem insurmountable, Jesus tells us that prayer and fasting are a vital means of solving them.

All fasting must go hand in hand with these abstentions from sin. We gain strength to move away from backbiting, carousing, lying, and an inordinate desire for material security. Above all, prayerful fasting can result in an increase of love of God and of neighbor.

Make sure your fasting doesn't damage your health. Before you attempt extended fasting, get the advice of a wise spiritual director.

Mary, Saints, and Angels

What is the meaning of the Catholic practice of canonizing saints?

When a person is "canonized," the church declares he or she is in heaven. The path a saint has taken to that goal is something Catholics can admire and perhaps imitate.

Being canonized a saint in the Catholic Church is not simple. Irrefutable miracles must be attributed to the person's intercession, and investigating the person's life makes for some pretty steep expenses. Usually the religious order to which the saint-to-be belonged puts up the money. This complicated process means that the saints in our world today probably won't ever be canonized. The daily bills are too big, and they probably will go to the grave with unpaid student loans.

The Catholic Church has fallen into a serious flaw in its teaching on holiness and the canonization of saints. Recently the pope canonized three priests. Then he canonized over a hundred Vietnamese martyrs and a holy nun who founded a religious community.

Now I don't object to people being declared saints. We need the example of outstanding people whose lives can help us to attain high levels of holiness.

Unfortunately nine out of ten canonized saints

have taken vows of celibacy or are martyrs—or both. I have no objection to celibacy. As a matter of fact, I've decided to live a celibate life myself. I certainly don't want to downplay martyrdom, either. If someone loves the Lord enough to surrender his or her life, he or she deserves all possible praise. My difficulty stems from the fact that 99 percent of Catholics don't have the least inclination toward celibacy or martyrdom.

With all their celibate/martyr saints, most Catholics think a high level of sanctity is just out of the question for them. The church fosters a "holiness inferiority complex" in its members. How can the mother of five ever attain to the church's ideal of holiness when she gets angry with her kids forty-seven times a day and is looking forward to having sex with her husband as often as possible? If we believe the message the church is giving by its canonizations, her sanctity would be acknowledged only if she were shot for going to Mass on Sunday or decided to enter a convent.

The Catholic Church must stop limiting the pursuit of holiness to something other than the joys and struggles that most people experience every day. A father who is making ends meet as a construction worker or taxing his wits each day in front of a computer can be just as holy as a monk in a mountaintop monastery. A young girl who wants more than anything in life to find a husband she can give all her love to can find holiness in her search. I am happy to say that the church is making efforts to correct this one-sided view of holiness. Bishops at the Second Vatican Council said that the striving for holiness doesn't require the taking of the vows of poverty, chastity, and obedience. Holiness can be found, they said, in any state of life.

The pope has seen the problem. In a letter on the laity, he called for the canonization of saints with whom the rank and file faithful can identify. The problem is that this official statement seems to be contradicted by his canonizing so many celibates and martyrs.

Someday I hope we will witness the canonization of Bill and Mary Smith who lived in Canoga Park, California, and raised five kids with a great deal of difficulty. They were preoccupied with dirty diapers, broken transmissions, sex education, getting laid off, Little League games, in-laws, and so on and on. When the kids married off, Mary decided to go back to school but had to work as a waitress to cover the cost of becoming a respiratory therapist. Bill worked in a factory till he retired at sixty-five. As their lives came to an end, they reflected that their greatest joys were raising their children, baby-sitting grandchildren, shopping, watching ball games, and making passionate love to each other.

In all of these "worldly" activities the Smiths developed a deep love for the Lord. They trusted in His love for them. They tried to pray to Him at least once a day as a family. They went to church each Sunday, but they seldom made it to daily Mass because they had too many other obligations. When Mary died of cancer at eighty-three, Bill was upset with God that He didn't treat her better. Bill died two years later. He loved and trusted God as best He could and wanted to be with Him and Mary for all eternity.

Saints Bill and Mary of Canoga Park, California,

as we live a life so similar to yours, "pray to God for us!"

What is this apparition of Mary at Fatima that some Catholics are so excited about?

On a pleasant May afternoon in 1917 three small children in a quiet, rustic village some one hundred miles north of Lisbon, Portugal, led their families' sheep to a grassy grove about two miles from their homes.

The ugly bloodletting of World War I in the rest of Europe had not touched this backward little hamlet.

Around noon while the children, ages seven to ten, were playing, they were startled by a crash of thunder. They ran to gather the sheep before the downpour began. Suddenly they saw a light hovering over one of the cork trees. They stopped. There was more than a light. There was a person, a breathtakingly beautiful woman, standing on the tree.

The woman spoke to the children, telling them that she was from heaven. "I want you to return to this spot each month for six months," she told them, "so I can share a special message with you."

The children decided not to tell anyone what they had seen. They knew they would be punished for even suggesting they had seen such a thing. But the youngest child, Jacinta, couldn't contain herself and had to share the secret. The parents were stern and incredulous.

On June 13 the lady appeared again. Soon word of the apparitions spread across the country. Thousands of people started to gather for the monthly occurrences. The forces of both faith and disbelief began to grow.

The children said that the purpose of Mary's visits was to call the world back to prayer, especially to the rosary. Penance was to be performed. If the world turned to prayer and penance, the Russian people would be converted from the atheism that was about to befall them.

At this time, the Bolshevik revolution had not been completed in Russia. It is miraculous that simple children in a backward country could know of this momentous future event.

On the last day of the apparitions, October 13, Mary promised a miracle that would help people to believe the children. In the presence of some seventy-thousand people, believers and atheists alike, the sun started to gyrate, giving off many colors. At one point, it seemed to start a plunge toward the earth. The miracle lasted for some ten minutes. Believers and unbelievers attested to this happening.

Do Catholics have to believe in such apparitions of Mary?

Catholics do *not* have to believe in these apparitions. The heart of what Catholics have to believe is found in the revelation given to us by Jesus Christ, which was handed down to us by word of mouth as well as through the inspired Scriptures.

Without obliging Catholics to believe in apparitions of Mary, the church in certain instances gives permission for Catholics to visit and pray at certain places where apparitions are said to have taken place. Many claimed apparitions of Mary have never received the Catholic Church's approval. Some of the better-known places that have been endorsed by the church as the sites of apparitions are Fatima, Portugal; Lourdes, France; and Guadalupe, Mexico.

Since the heart of all revelation came with Jesus, the Catholic Church is very slow to lend credence to purported apparitions of Jesus and the saints. Jesus doesn't need to give us more information. If there are apparitions, they are to encourage us to be more faithful to the revelation already given. If these apparitions call people to a deeper commitment to the Lord and the church, I'm inclined to give credence to them. Church permission to Catholics to visit these places as official places of prayer came after many years of scrutiny and the confirmation of indisputable miracles. I have visited Fatima and Guadalupe and found my faith in Jesus strengthened.

Why do Catholics give so much attention to Mary, the mother of Jesus? She often seems to get more attention than her Son.

Whenever Catholics speak of their devotion to Mary, the ground rules must be clear: Mary is nothing without Jesus! In herself, Mary is no more than you and I. Her greatness comes from the blessings God has given her.

The basis of any discussion of Mary needs to come from the words she tells her cousin Elizabeth, "My soul proclaims the greatness of the Lord; my spirit rejoices in God my savior. For he has looked upon his handmaid's lowliness; behold, from now on will all ages call me blessed. The mighty One has done great things for me, and holy is his name" (Luke 1:46–49).

A distorted attention to Mary may come from a theology that stresses Jesus' divinity and undermines His humanity. When Jesus becomes a distant judge whose main concern is justice, we lose touch with His balance of tender humanity. He embraced children lovingly, forgave the woman caught in adultery, and begged His Father to let the cup of suffering pass from Him.

When Jesus is seen as a judgmental, distant God, some Catholics ask His mother to intercede. She knows how to get past His strictness. She can soften His heart.

Now is that way of thinking wrong? Most certainly. It is heresy. Catholics are wrong when they say, "As children who didn't know how to approach our father for a favor, we went to our mother who knew how to talk to Dad. So we go to Mary." That approach is fraught with difficulties of practically saying Mary is more important to approach than Jesus.

Some Catholics spend more time developing a relationship with Mary than with Jesus. I suppose that if you pushed these devotees to question their devotion to Mary, they would deny that Mary is more important than Jesus.

Why did Catholics begin to venerate Mary?

When we look to Scripture, we find that in the early church there were diverse understandings of Mary similar to what we find among many Catholics and protestants today. The community out of which Mark wrote gave little attention to Mary. As a matter of fact, many statements about her seem to be negative. In the third chapter, we first meet Mary as a mother who wants to take Jesus away from His public ministry. With all Jesus' preaching and healing, He is not taking time to eat. Word is out that He is insane.

When we come to the gospel of Luke, we find much more devotion to Mary. Luke does not mention her concern for Jesus' sanity. Instead, he brings in the annunciation and Mary's submission to the Lord's challenge. The Magnificat claims, to the delight of most Catholics, that "all generations will call me blest because He who is mighty has done great things for me."

The same diverse attention given to Mary by Catholics and certain protestants today mirrors the diversity of importance given Mary in the Gospels of Mark and Luke.

If Mary could speak to us now about the division between many protestants and Catholics, I am confident she would beg Catholics not to make her a red flag to wave in the face of others who don't share devotion to her. Mary loves Jesus completely, and she is not going to become indignant if she is ignored and her Son is given prominence.

I can't see Mary as anything more than a fine example from the past. Catholics act as if she's still alive.

Catholics believe that Mary, like all the faithful who have died and are with the Lord, is alive. Death for the faithful does not mean they are put on ice until the Second Coming. For Catholics, the sleep of the faithful, which Paul speaks about ("For if we believe that Jesus died and rose, so too will

God, through Jesus, bring with him those who have fallen asleep" (1 Thess. 4:14), is not some kind of comatose state. We are alive in a vital and real way to the Lord and to all those who are living on the earth. The life we have in the Holy Spirit on this earth doesn't end. That common life enables us to be united with all those who share the Spirit.

For Catholics, this relationship is called the Communion of Saints—a spiritual communion between those in heaven and on earth. Because God "is not God of the dead, but of the living, for to him all are alive" (Luke 20:38), we are all united. That means that my mom, who is now with the Lord, can be someone I can turn to and ask to go to the Lord to intercede for me. She sees the Lord face to face.

That doesn't mean that we can't go directly to the Lord with our needs. That is vitally important in any relationship with Him. But we are also urged to come to Him with and through others.

If this life of the saints in heaven is real and we share this life, not only do we ask them to intercede for us but we also are able to develop relationships with them. They are living persons; we are living persons. We share a common life. We can have friends in heaven—like Mary!

Now wait a minute. Scripture says that there is only one mediator—Jesus!

Of course there is only one mediator, Jesus, the Son of God. Without denying that truth I can also say that the Holy Spirit intercedes for us with inexpressible groanings (Rom. 8:28). Paul also asks the Thessalonians to pray for him (2 Thess. 3:1–2)

and says that he prays for them (2 Thess. 1:11).
Aren't these acts of mediation?

Most Christians have little difficulty in asking
others to pray for them and in turn promising to
pray for others. Such acts of prayer do not deny
that Jesus is the one mediator. Instead, our
friends' prayers stress our union with each other
as we support each other in prayer. We come together to one Mediator.

I don't like the idea of relationships with spirits. Isn't it unbiblical?

I find the fostering of relationships with Mary
and the saints a joyful gift from the Lord. I can
have a happy relationship with an outstanding
person who is a hero in the struggle to follow the
Lord. I can turn to people I admire who are in the
Bible: Abraham, Moses, David, Mary, Peter, and
Paul. They and I share a common life and love for
the Lord.

A saint by the name of Anthony lived in a town
in Italy called Padua several hundred years ago. I
ask him to intercede for me frequently when I have
lost something. Am I sounding silly? God blesses
friendship, and He delights in friends coming to
Him together to know Him, love Him, and seek His
help. He cares about us when we need to choose
the direction for our lives as well as when we wonder where we have misplaced a watch.

I don't mean that we should dialogue with them
at seances! When I talk with them, I don't expect to
hear their voices any more than I expect to hear
the actual voice of the Lord. In my faith, I believe
that saints are alive and their response to my pray-

ing can come through a stirring in my soul or a favor granted.

I get the image of King Saul conjuring up evil spirits with the witches of Endor.

I don't want to minimize the danger of dealing with evil spirits. But if my experience of a person living on the earth or if people I trust affirm a person, I know that a person has lived a life worthy of gaining eternal life. I shouldn't exclude a relationship with him or her because there might be evil spirits. Isn't that the extreme of a parent who won't allow a child to have good friends because there are so many possible bad friends out there?

This is foreign to me. I still have problems with others getting in the way of my direct relationship with the Lord.

Look at it this way. If you are married, is it fair to ask if you love your spouse? I hope you will say that you love that person very much. You will even confirm that your partner is a gift from the Lord. God blesses your love.

God wants us to come to Him through relationships with other people. An unhealthy person says, "I am going to do away with all relationships with others so that I can have only a relationship with God." No, family, friends, and even enemies are an integral part of our relationship with God. Jesus tells us that we must love God *and* our neighbor.

Loving others doesn't mean that we love God less. Even my life as a celibate must be integrally tied into the lives of my family, my friends, and even my enemies.

Because I believe that those who have died in the Lord are alive, I have no problem with turning to them to ask that they intercede with the Lord just as I ask my friends that I can see to pray to the Lord for me. Our love for the Lord isn't diminished by loving others, including those who have gone before us to heaven.

What is the rosary?

The rosary has a history that goes back to the twelfth century. Initially it had 150 beads in imitation of the 150 Psalms from the Bible. Today a rosary ordinarily has sixty beads on which the prayer "Hail Mary" is said ten times. Then there is a special bead for saying an "Our Father."

This is the Hail Mary: "Hail Mary, full of grace, the Lord is with you. Blessed are you among women and blessed is the fruit of your womb, Jesus. Holy Mary, Mother of God, pray for us sinners now and at the hour of our death. Amen."

The first half of this prayer is taken from the Gospel of Luke using the words of the angel Gabriel and Elizabeth. The second half of the prayer requests that Mary go to the Lord in prayer for us.

The rosary is a meditation on Jesus and His revelation.

The Catholic bishops of the United States recently encouraged Catholics to pray the rosary. They suggested using images from the Scripture as themes for meditation while saying the rosary.

Now, I think you are definitely going against Jesus when you pray with such repetition. Jesus warns against such rattling on in Matthew 6:7.

I agree completely. If saying the rosary is a mindless rattling of repetitive prayers, then forget it. On the other hand, if it is a means of prayerful meditation on the mysteries of salvation, its recitation should be encouraged.

To me, Mary is the most beautiful example of a person who has surrendered herself to Jesus. I am honored to join her in prayer.

For me the repetition of the rosary is not deadening but comparable to the repetition of a musical theme in a great symphony. Such repetition is the key to the power of the piece of music, which has the ability to take me to a deeper awareness of myself. There is beauty in the repetition. The music opens my spirit to higher aspirations.

The rosary is such a symphony to me. In the repetitions of the words of Scripture and the petitions, I come to a deeper experience of Jesus and His love for me.

Prayerful repetition can be found in the Psalms, which were favorite prayers of Jesus. In Psalm 136 the phrase "for His mercy endures forever" is repeated twenty-six times. This is not empty rattling but a means of raising our spirits to the Lord.

Do you believe that Mary was always a virgin? In my Bible Jesus has brothers and sisters.

A strong tradition, which was established by Christians in the early church, says that Mary was

93

a virgin, both before and after the birth of Jesus.

The problem arises from translations of Matthew 13:55–56 and Matthew 12:46, which speak of Jesus' "brothers and sisters." These Greek words can mean near or remote brethren or relatives. In both Hebrew and western Aramaic (the language used by Jesus), there was no specific word for cousin, uncle, aunt. Near kinsfolk were referred to as brothers and sisters, especially in the extended or patriarchal family of the time.

There are examples of the confusion in the Hebrew Bible: Lot was Abraham's brother's son (Gen. 12:5), yet Abraham called him "brother" (13:8). Tobias called his second cousin, Sara, his "sister" several times (Tobit 8:4,7).

Jesus' four "brothers" are mentioned by name in Matthew 13:55: James, Joseph (Joses), Simon, and Judas (Jude). Certainly James and Joseph (Joses) were not sons of Mary, the mother of Jesus, since they are listed as sons of another Mary (the "other Mary" mentioned in Matt. 27:61) at the foot of the cross in Matthew 27:56 and Mark 15:40. Yet James and Joseph are listed as "brothers" of Jesus. This is an example of the semantic confusion that leads to the conclusion that Christ had siblings, contrary to the consistent tradition from the early church, which held these "brothers and sisters" to be Jesus' "brethren."

The assumption of the blessed Virgin Mary is hard for me to accept. Do Catholics believe she is some goddess?

She is as completely human as we are, not some sort of demigod. The doctrine of the Assumption of Mary in no way detracts from her total humanity;

CATHOLIC SPIRITUALITY

it simply states that after she finished her life on earth, she was taken body and soul to heaven. Mary's assumption is a truth revealed by God not in Scripture but in the early teachings and writing of the leaders who followed the apostles.

Many fundamental Christians talk of the Rapture, when, at the Second Coming, we will be taken up to heaven. This doctrine of the Assumption of Mary is a beautiful foretaste of our physical resurrection and union with Jesus. What God accomplished for Mary is also our hope.

Do Catholics believe in guardian angels?

We read of the work of angels throughout the Bible. In Psalm 91:11 the psalmist speaks of guardian angels "guarding you in all your ways." In Matthew 18:10 Jesus speaks of the guardian angels who have charge over children. In Revelation we read of angels who are guardians of various cities.

Catholics believe that angels are supernatural beings created by God long before our world was created. Our guardian angels watch over us and care for us.

When I was in first grade in Catholic school, I was encouraged to give my guardian angel a name. I chose Timothy. With great simplicity, I left space for him on my classroom seat. It's a shame that I think so infrequently of Tim now!

I believe it is important for us to communicate with guardian angels frequently. However, we tend to get a little nervous when we deal with things we can't see and touch. So it is with the mystery of angels. Through the eyes of faith we know that there are heavenly creatures praising God and doing His work right now. As our awareness of their presence grows, we should join with them in one beautiful chorus of praise to our Lord.

Satan

What do you know about the devil?

The Scriptures tell us that before his fall, the devil was a glorious angel—Lucifer, the light bearer. His pride caused him to turn away from God, and he was cast out of heaven forever. We believe God allows him to move about in the world. Because of this, we need to be aware of him and continually invoke the power of Jesus to overcome anything Satan might do.

As Christians we need not be fearful of him as long as we are incorporated in Christ. Jesus conquered Satan on the cross. No matter how cunning Lucifer is, we have victory in Jesus: "For there is one greater in you than there is in the world" (1 John 4:4).

What about demon possession?

The Scriptures tell us of the reality of demons, yet these demonic spirits do not ordinarily work in the astonishing manner the film *The Exorcist* depicts. Rather, with Satan at their helm, they generally move in people's lives in seemingly insignificant ways.

One of their greatest schemes is to get us to worry about the past or future so that the individual takes his eyes off God. God has said His name is "I Am Who I Am"—not a God who was or will be, but a God of power in this present moment. Anxiety about the past and future is one of Satan's most clever tools. It keeps us from living in the power and beauty of what God wants for us right now.

The Catholic Church still believes in the office of *exorcist,* the ministry of praying and fasting for someone who has been possessed by Satan. I received the order of exorcist as one of the steps to my ordination to the priesthood. The church has given me the power to drive out Satan through laying on hands and praying for someone. Ordinarily this happens every time I baptize someone. I tell Satan, if he is present, to leave the person.

Today priests do not receive the office of exorcist on the road to ordination. This function is reserved for especially holy people who are appointed by the bishop of a diocese to administer the rite of exorcism to a possessed person.

Satan is real. Possessions of people by him are real. Jesus deals with possession eight times in the Scriptures. He commissions his disciples to drive out Satan. Satan has an intelligence that is higher than our human reasoning. He has the power to possess people. When a possession takes place, a person isn't necessarily guilty of sin. The rite of exorcism calls Satan out of a person through prayer and fasting and doesn't imply that a person has sinned. Satan cannot force a person to do something morally wrong. Despite his higher intellect, we still have the freedom of choice.

A bishop who is presented with a purported case of demon possession will not act quickly. There are too many possibilities that the signs of possession are merely mental or physical disturbances. Only after he is assured that there is a demonic possession will he call on the exorcist.

A good book to read concerning Satan is *The*

Screwtape Letters, by C. S. Lewis. Remember, the power of Jesus, His body and His blood, is all we need to overcome Satan.

Religious Communities

What are religious communities like the Jesuits, Benedictines, and Franciscans?

I am certain that to those who know of Catholicism only from the outside, such words as *Jesuit, Benedictine,* and *Franciscan* are filled with all kinds of mystery.

Actually, these words are the names of groups of Catholics who have banded together to serve special needs that have arisen in the church.

Benedictines follow a man by the name of Benedict, who lived around the year 500. This highly educated man followed the example of many early monks in Asia Minor and formed communities for prayer and study. He is credited with beginning the education system in Europe, a system that later came to the Americas. There was a need for education, and Benedict responded to the need.

Franciscans are men and women who have been inspired to follow Jesus more closely under the inspiration of St. Francis of Assisi. Back in the thirteenth century Francis, who was from a rich family, heard Jesus call him to a greater love of the poor. He let go of wealth and the desire for worldly status. He got his food and shelter by begging from others. Thus stripped of material need, he was free to preach Jesus and find God's beauty in animals and the beauties of nature. Today several thousand men and women are striving to attain Francis' detachment from material goods and find their strength in the Lord. Francis' message then and now is a challenge to depend on God rather than material wealth.

Jesuits were founded shortly after Luther and the other reformers made their break with the Catholic Church. Catholics found themselves needing to respond to the criticisms of the protestants. A Spaniard by the name of Ignatius decided to leave his life as a soldier and dedicate himself to explaining Catholic beliefs. Ignatius also heard God call him to send missionaries to places around the world where Christ was not known. And so Ignatius' dream of bringing Christ to others moved to universities in Europe, and Jesuit missionaries went out to India, China, Japan, South America, and even to our United States.

I am a member of a similar community called the *Society of the Divine Word.* We were founded in 1875 by a German priest named Arnold Janssen. He heard Christ's call to send missionaries around the world. Today we number fifty-five hundred members and work in over fifty countries. Janssen was committed to the use of mass media, to share Christ's love with others. In our evangelization today we make great use of the printed word and the electronic media.

If a Catholic feels called to join one of these religious communities, there are hundreds of such communities to choose from, even some communities for married couples to join. The places a community works range from hospitals or universities to slums or parishes.

A person goes though several years of discernment before making a lifelong commitment to a community.

What about these contemplative Catholics who close themselves off from the world to pray?

I deeply admire people who are called to serve God with a strong stress on prayer. They are striving for a high level of surrender to the Lord in their lives.

I understand their lives in the context of Paul's image of the body of Christ. Paul speaks of a head, a hand, and a foot. Different parts of a body have different functions, but each is still one with the whole body. And so contemplatives are a special part of the body of Christ whose function is to spend a great deal of time in praise of God and prayer for the needs of the world.

Contemplatives are not shut off from the world. In many ways they are more attuned to the vitally important aspects of our life than are we who are often distracted.

The contemplatives I know are very balanced, bright, loving, and full of joy. I hope that more and more men and women choose this beautiful way of giving their lives to God.

What are the vows of poverty, chastity, and obedience that members of these communities take?

The commitment to a religious community like the Jesuits or Benedictines involves taking three vows. With the vows a person gives up ownership of all personal possessions, agrees not to marry, and follows the directions of those chosen to be leaders.

This style of commitment to Christ is quite radical. It comes from a desire to follow closely the example of Jesus' life. In the Gospels we hear of Christ calling us to give up all material things and be dependent on God. Jesus lived the life of a celibate and was obedient to His Father's will.

Please explain more about the vows.

Obedience. When a person takes a vow he or she doesn't surrender intelligence and common sense. The practical reason for obedience is the forming of community. When different people come together to form a community, a natural inclination toward selfishness must be curbed to foster the common good.

The same principle is alive in society. If I selfishly break the law by stealing or by running red lights, I disrupt the general order. I must submit my selfish desires to serve the common good.

Yet comparing the vow of obedience to complying with laws in society isn't completely correct. The analogy limps. There is a presence of the Lord in the decisions of a superior with the community.

Nevertheless, because I have a God-given intelligence, if a superior makes a decision with which I don't agree, I am obliged to discuss the issue with him. If, after that dialogue, the superior and the community disagree with my view, I should conform to their decision unless doing so would be sinful.

Poverty. Jesus offers a strong challenge to our modern affluent society. I hear this challenge in Jesus' words to the rich young man who came to Him wanting to know what he had to do to gain eternal life. Jesus enumerated the commandments. The young man had kept them since his youth. "Jesus, looking at him loved him and said to him 'You are lacking in one thing. Go sell what you have, and give to the poor and you will have treasure in heaven; then come, follow me" (Mark 10:22). At this, the young man's face fell, and he went away sad, for he had many possessions.

Jesus calls some people to this radical surrender of material things. The vow of poverty is a response to Christ's invitation to make sure that our security in life is in God's strength rather than material possessions.

Although I've taken a vow of poverty, in imitation of Christ's poverty, I live the vow with many more things than Jesus had as He walked the hills of Galilee. I have given up ownership of anything and strive to be detached from the computer, the car, and the credit cards I use to do my work. Others who take the vow of poverty make a more radical surrender of material things.

The heart of the vow is a spirit of simplicity of lifestyle, detachment from material possessions, and a strong dependence on God for what is necessary.

Celibacy. Scripture tells us that Christ chose not to be married. In Matthew 19:12 Jesus speaks of those, like Himself, who turn away from marriage for the kingdom of God. To choose such a radical call today is a very extreme style of life. This way of living contrasts with the cavalier attitude toward illicit sex that is touted through much of media. Only with God's support can a person live a loving life of celibacy.

Celibacy offers freedom from family obligations to concentrate on a personal relationship with the Lord. This freedom from family ties also makes the celibate available to serve the needs of the larger Christian community.

Because celibacy involves a radical imitation of Jesus' lifestyle, some have argued that celibacy is better than marriage. A look through church history shows that some celibates have even wanted to do away with marriage for everyone. Celibacy must always be seen as a personal call from God in the same way that marriage is a call from God. Celibates and those married should not fall into pettiness and claim one lifestyle is better than the other.

Celibacy is good because God asks a person to live that style of life. Marriage is good because God asks a person to embrace that life. We should eliminate the word *better* when evaluating God's call. Not to do so leads to paternalism on the part of those who favor celibacy over marriage.

Isn't it very difficult to choose a life of celibacy?

Logic is not the best way to explain celibacy. For me, this call from the Lord is quite mysterious. I know that this state of life is not for everyone. My attraction to celibacy is first of all a gift from the Lord. With my natural attraction to marriage and its intimacy, I need the Lord's help to remain faithful to my commitment.

One can choose celibacy in various ways. I made a final choice of it when I was twenty-eight years old, just before I was ordained a priest. Prior to that I had made one-year commitments to celibacy for five years. I had a chance to evaluate celibacy during five years of temporary commitment before making a lifelong commitment.

A lay person might choose celibacy in a quiet, private decision. A homosexual could choose it. A person who loses a marriage partner might choose celibacy. Celibacy can be a rich way of loving and serving others and reaching a high level of fulfillment.

I find the commitment to celibacy can be very difficult at times of loneliness and failure. I can imagine that a married man knows the same pull to unfaithfulness when he doesn't get the love he feels he needs from his wife.

Celibacy becomes fruitful when the force of sexuality in a person is directed toward serving the needy in the world. That is very fulfilling. The value of celibacy is not found in its negation of marriage but rather in its freeing the celibate for great service and love.

Despite the challenge of living celibate, I am glad that I have made this commitment. I ask the Lord to protect me in my resolve. I wish that celibacy had better P.R. We Catholic priests and religious should generate a more joyful and positive image of the celibate.

Jesus says I should leave everything and follow Him. I don't understand such surrender.

We know what it means to give up things for some goal. Marriage means we give up a life of independence to concentrate on a partner and the children who come from that love. Much is sacrificed to make the marriage work.

We see this giving of self in a person who strives to be a success in business. After many years of study there are further years of apprenticeship and struggle. When victory can be seen, the pain of single-minded dedication is secondary to the goal of success.

The call of Christ to give up everything in order to love Him totally is similar, yet even more complete. His sweeping demand of total surrender to His love seems a bit more than I can handle.

At one point He says, "Whoever wishes to come after me must deny himself, take up his cross, and follow me. For whoever wishes to save his life will lose it, but whoever loses his life for my sake and that of the gospel will save it" (Mark 8:34–35). He wants us to be as courageous, loving, and willing to suffer injustice as He was. My laziness and desire for comfort rebel at such giving.

If this weren't enough, another time He says, "If your foot causes you to sin, cut it off" (Mark 9:45). If my hand or my foot or my eye gets in the way of the love between us, I should cut off that hand and foot and gouge out that eye rather than cause my love to be compromised.

That certainly is radical! The problem is that this tremendous Lover doesn't stop there. He even asks that I give up more. He tells me to give up my worry, to trust in Him for my food, my clothes, my peace—everything (Luke 12:22ff).

How unreasonable of Him to think that I should go through life without the anxiety and apprehension that seem such a natural part of living in this world.

This surrender is to be made to Him in the quiet of my heart. I must admit that He is real. I must believe that He is God. I must believe that He loves me at this very moment no matter how tangled I am in sin. I must believe that this love we have will go on for all eternity.

Such a surrender is difficult. Yet even more difficult is Christ's request that I make my love concrete through the care I give to the people who are part of my life. Love for Jesus is integrally tied to love of husband, wife, children, of the illegal immigrant, the depressed widow, the bigot, the rude teenager, and the person who demands more of me than I think I should give.

Is so much sacrifice and surrender worth it? To someone who hasn't taken the plunge into Christ's love, it remains a frightening and painful risk. But to someone who has said, "Yes!" to Christ, to surrender to Him, no matter how incomplete, is the key to deep peace, joy, meaning, and love.

Am I disqualified from being a Christian because I have a car, a house, and credit cards? Should I forget about my wife and children's needs?

We need to strike a balance in understanding Christ's words about giving up everything and following Him. If we had never heard about Jesus and then picked up the Gospel of Luke, the Jesus we would meet would ask of us that total surrender. Is that for everyone?

What does that mean to the couple raising five children? Both are working to pay for the house and food and for modest entertainment. Does Jesus want them to give up everything? Yes, some people are to give up everything. Some need not do that. In that Gospel of Luke we find that Zacchaeus is challenged to give up only half of what he possesses. And what about the women who financed the missionary work of Jesus and the apostles? If they had given up everything, they wouldn't have been able to help Jesus' company of disciples financially. Another example of the balance of giving up possessions comes at the Last Supper in Luke's account. Whereas Jesus had told the apostles to go out preaching with only the clothes they had, now He says to them, "When I sent you forth without a money bag or a sack or sandals, were you in need of anything?" "No, nothing," they replied. He said to them, "But now one who has a money bag should take it, and likewise a sack, and one who does not have a sword should sell his cloak and buy one" (Luke 22:35–36).

Far be it from me to water down Christ's radical call. He may be speaking to you of a surrender that I would not want to hold back. Still and all, make sure you hear Christ's call for balance. Whether you give up all you possess and go to a monastery or are blessed with great wealth, strive to be dependent on Him in all matters by continually giving to those in need.

Wrestling with God

How can you say God is loving when there are so many tragedies in our lives?

My belief in God can sometimes be shaken when He allows things to happen that are contrary to my expectations of a loving God. How can a God of forgiveness, love, and compassion allow an airplane collision or an earthquake or a hurricane, which results in the horrifying death of so many people?

We can choose to reject Him in the face of the overwhelming carnage: "If God exists and if He cared, He could have somehow caused one of the pilot's hands to move or the hurricane to blow into a harmless area. We could have had a near tragedy. Instead we were horrified, shocked, hurt. People lost family members and friends."

Our disillusionment with God is similar to our disappointment when a friend or relative doesn't live up to our expectations. We might have believed in that person until we were surprised to catch him in a lie or in an act of unfaithfulness. We can reject the person by renouncing our faith in him because of our damaged expectations. Or we can admit that our expectations were unrealistic and continue believing in him but with a more truthful eye.

Rather than turn away from God, I would like to reevaluate my expectations of Him to understand Him better through such happenings. In the face of murder, injustice, or hundreds of deaths in a plane crash or an earthquake, logic and reason are stretched beyond their limits. Although I think God is all-powerful, somehow He curtails His power. Although I believe in God's love, I concede to a mystery beyond my understanding in some of His actions.

If you watched someone you love very much writhing to death with the constant pain of vaginal cancer, would you honestly look to the Source of life and the Sustainer of creation with love?

The worst way to respond to you would be with some impersonal cliché about how God especially loves those who suffer or that your loved one's pain is part of the pain of the mystical body and is joined with the pain of Christ for the world's redemption.

You don't need to hear the words "God still cares" because, for all practical purposes, God has abandoned you and the one you love. You don't even need me to tell you that I understand because I have had a similar experience.

All I want to do is remain silent and cry with you.

Will I ever be able to see God as loving in the midst of my anger and loss?

Belief in a loving God is not a matter of logic or of reading something that will make Him seem loving to us. Belief in a loving God is a matter of receiving the gift of faith, something that I cannot generate myself. God will give me the eyes to see His love if I am willing to receive it.

God's love has touched me with an ineffable experience of His forgiveness and acceptance of me whenever I have asked forgiveness of Him and His community in telling sins to a priest in the Sacrament of Reconciliation. Hand in hand with that experience is the image of Jesus dying on the cross. As I look at Jesus, the Son of God, hanging on the cross, my faith stirs.

Jesus on the cross is the greatest sign of absurdity, injustice, and misguided freedom the world has ever known. In seeing my Savior on the cross, I hear him say to me, "Michael, I wish that you could be freed from all of life's absurdity, injustice, sickness, and death. But sin has left this scar on creation. My response is My death on the cross. I am reaching out to share your pain. In this love of your God for you, may you have hope, even in the teeth of Beirut, Dachau, and the deaths of those you love.

"I do not choose to eliminate pain, suffering, and injustice. I do choose to become one with you in your struggle with the absurd. I was the most loving and caring person in the world. How did the world respond to me? It killed me in a cruel way. You can understand my physical, emotional, and spiritual pain.

"Look at me on the cross and know that I love you. I cry with you. Certainly that isn't the whole answer. You will never fully understand why I permit suffering in the world, but look at me as one with you in your suffering.

"Hold on. I promise a victory. I promise life that will never end. I do promise you the full answer."

The End Times

Do Catholics believe in the second coming of Jesus?

Yes, most assuredly Catholics believe our Lord is coming again. We remind ourselves of this belief every time we attend Mass, we pray for the Lord's coming in the Creed, when we repeat the words "Christ has died, Christ has risen, Christ will come again." After the words of consecration of the bread and wine into Christ's body and blood. And after the recital of the Our Father we pray, "As we wait in joyful hope for the coming of our Savior Jesus Christ."

Our attitude toward the second coming should be similar to the feelings of a long distance runner. He's run for twenty-five long, hot miles, but suddenly, with the finish line in sight, he's able to sprint. He has the energy because he knows the end is near. We should have the same excitement and expectations for the coming of our Lord. We needn't worry about saving enough energy for to-morrow; the Lord is near and we must do all we can right now to usher in the fullness of His King-dom through the grace God gives us.

Do Catholics believe in the Antichrist?

The word *antichrist* occurs in the New Testa-ment only in 1 John 2:18,22, 4:3; and in 2 John 7 and 2 Thessalonians 2, where it is used as a well-known term. This figure's war against God will reach its peak just before the great final judgment.

A similar figure appears in Revelation 11:7, the beast which comes out of the abyss, and in 13:1– 10, the beast which comes from the sea, uttering blasphemies and conquering the earth. This beast is followed by another beast, number 666, which performs wonders and makes men worship the first beast. The beasts are connected with the "Scarlet Woman" of 17:1, who is a thinly disguised personification of Rome. The pictures of the beasts are derived from Daniel 7:1.

Most Catholics are not of the opinion that the Antichrist is a real historical-eschatological figure. In Revelation the connection of the beast with the Roman Empire which persecuted the church is too close. The number 666 has been figured to be the sum of the numerical value of the Hebrew letters of the name Caesar Nero (KSR NRWN).

The allusions in 1 and 2 John speak of many antichrists. Anyone who denies Jesus is anti-christ. Antichrist is rather a personification of the powers of evil which occasionally focus in some individual person and can be expected to do so again.

Is the Roman Catholic Church the Antichrist?

To say the least, this is a disturbing question for Catholics. No, the Roman Catholic Church is not the Antichrist. It seems that this very negative image of the church comes from transferring the bad things said of the Roman Empire in the Book of Revelation to the Roman Church.

Why do some people use the book of Revelation (Apocalypse) to scare people into coming to God?

Jesus certainly preached strong words to people who had wandered far from the will of His Father: "Things that cause sin will inevitably occur, but woe to the person through whom they occur. It would be better for him if a millstone were put around his neck and he be thrown into the sea than for him to cause one of these little ones to sin" (Luke 17:1–2). Such preaching has its place today. But such fury must be aimed at the people who really need it. To indiscriminately try to scare people is a gross misuse of God's good news.

That is why I am often repulsed by the practice of using the calamity-ridden creatures in the Book of Revelation to call people to the Lord. When preachers and teachers pin down a prophecy in Revelation and insist dogmatically that it is being fulfilled in current world events, I get nervous because I see this as a fear tactic. Although the aim of such an interpretation is to warn those not responding to the Lord, often these "prophets" are preaching a fearsome God to people who don't deserve to be so frightened. As a youth I was troubled by this picture of an "awful" God, and it has caused years of unnecessary suffering for me. Many Christians have gone through the same pain.

Jesus calls us to peace. As long as we are trying to do good, He will be patient with us. I see God's call to conversion in the spirit of the prodigal son's father, who waited in loving forbearance.

SECTION 3

The Seven Sacraments

The sacraments are signs of an encounter with Jesus Christ in the church community. Let me explain the word sacrament. When we try to express something that is in our hearts, the only way we can do so is through words, objects, or physical action—signs of something more. If a husband loves his wife, he expresses that love through words, actions, and things. He says "I love you." He kisses her. Then he gives her a bouquet of flowers. All are symbols of a love that can never be fully expressed.

Jesus has a great love for us, and because of our material and physical makeup, He expresses that love with signs and symbols. The Seven Sacraments involve the use of words, actions, and material things. They are sacred because they represent God reaching out to touch us and embrace us with His tenderness. Some of the things used are water, clothes, oil, candles, food, and actions like the laying on of hands.

The sacraments are even more than signs. They are encounters with God at the key moments of our lives.

What are these Seven Sacraments that seem so important to Catholics?

Baptism is the celebration of God's presence in the person. He or she becomes an official member of the Christian community.

Confirmation is an experience of God's power when as teenagers we struggle to make our faith our own after having been taught by family and teachers. The anointing that accompanies confirmation was originally part of the baptismal ceremony. This anointing was separated from Baptism so that the local bishop, when he visited the parish, would be able to have a role in baptisms. As years passed, the episcopal anointing "became" the Sacrament of Confirmation.

Reconciliation means we are reconciled to the Christian community we have harmed by our sins.

In the *Eucharist*, we find the strength we need for life's struggles. In it we find fraternity with Christ and the community with whom we share the Bread of Life.

Marriage is celebrated when spouses surrender their love and life in commitment to one another under God's guidance in the church. Marriage in a church is a celebration of several things: the couple's commitment to each other, God's commitment to their love, the parish community's commitment to the couple, and the couple's commitment to the community.

Holy Orders is a call to servant leadership in the church. Catholics call their leaders *priests* because they preside at Mass, a renewal of the one sacrifice of Jesus on Calvary.

Catholics believe that all the baptized persons are "members of a royal priesthood," but the ordained priest is to be a leader in the community, especially at the celebration of the Mass and of the Sacrament of Reconciliation.

The Sacrament of the Sick shows forth God's loving care by reaching out to the sick with words and actions of concern, forgiveness, and healing.

Each sacrament celebrates God's presence with us. Too often we take His presence and love for granted. Through the sacraments, the church offers us the chance to celebrate His love at key moments of our lives from infancy to death.

Are the sacraments based on Scripture or tradition or both?

References to all the Catholic sacraments can be found in Scripture:

- Jesus told his followers to baptize (Matt. 29:19).
- Confirmation, which has a close connection to the Sacrament of Baptism, highlights the coming of the Holy Spirit. John the Baptist says, "I am baptizing you with water, but one mightier than I is coming. I am not worthy to loosen the thongs of his sandals. He will baptize you with the Holy Spirit and fire" (Luke 3:16).
- Jesus gave authority to His disciples to forgive

sins: "He breathed on them and said to them, "Receive the Holy Spirit. Whose sins you forgive are forgiven them, and whose sins you retain are retained" (John 20:22–23).

- The celebration of the Eucharist is done because of Christ's command at the Last Supper to do what He did (Luke 22:19).
- The office of priesthood also related to Christ's commission at the Last Supper. The apostles were called on to do what priests now do: offer what seems bread and wine but in reality is the body and blood of Christ offered once on Calvary. That one sacrifice is made present each time the priest offers the Eucharist (Matt. 26:26–28).
- Paul says marriage is a symbol of Christ's love for the church (Eph. 5:21–33).
- Finally, James writes of elders coming to anoint the sick (James 5:14–15).

Through the years the rituals connected with the sacraments have taken various forms. For example, the Jewish Passover structure of the Last Supper has been influenced by the various cultures where Christianity has taken root. Through the years, prayers and actions have been added to the basic sacrament.

Baptism

Why do Catholics baptize infants?

When the Catholic Church asks that infants be baptized, it sees faith and grace as gifts from God and not something we generate on our own. Infant baptism also recognizes the community to which the infant is integrally tied. The faith of the parents, godparents, and local church community are part of the infant's faith.

The greatest drawback to infant baptism is that persons so baptized may think they don't have to grow in their faith through the years. This sacrament is only a beginning. There is a need for continual renewal of one's commitment. Although God's grace is unfailing, we must respond with love for God and others all through our lives.

What is "original sin"?

St. Paul says that Christ restored what Adam and Eve had lost, clearly implying that all human beings once had and somehow lost a gracious intimacy with God through that first or "original" sin of Adam.

Once Adam and Eve made their choice to reject God's invitation to intimacy and union, certain possibilities for humankind were closed. Only in Christ could they be reopened. The Catholic Church has never defined the nature of this original sin, its time, or its circumstance.

The Council of Trent said this sin is a true sin that is present in every human being. We all receive the sin at birth, distinct from sins we commit as we grow older. The effects of the sin are the loss of justice and holiness, and the incurrence of divine wrath and death.

We humans imitate Adam's sin by our personal sin; but from birth we are affected by original sin. I understand this sin when I feel an inclination to hurt even someone I love. I see it in a nation that can get caught up in injustice and murder like in Nazi Germany or Cambodia.

Christ is the answer to overcoming this terrible

sin. The sacraments and especially baptism speak of a victory over original sin. But this victory is not simply accomplished. We have to do battle with the help of God's grace against the effects of original sin. Like the kingdom, the victory is here and now, but not yet.

What is this "limbo" you Catholics believe unbaptized babies go to?

Limbo was a place where the souls of unbaptized babies went after death. This place was neither heaven nor hell. For nearly a thousand years after Christ there apparently was little concern about where unbaptized infants went when they died. It simply was assumed that God took care of these children in His own way.

Various theologians differed and argued about the subject, but the universal church took no official position. Only in the eighteenth century did the question become critical. A heretical European sect called Jansenists held extremely severe positions about morality and grace. One of their doctrines was that according to God's revelation, all infants dying without baptism were condemned to the fires of hell. Belief in any kind of limbo, they said, was to be condemned.

Eight years later in 1794, Pope Pius VI condemned the teaching of Jansenists. One may believe in a limbo, a place of happiness that is not heaven, and still be a Catholic.

This is the only statement on Limbo in all major official documents of the church. The church never has and does not now endorse or reject the existence of such a "place."

Given those options, I think the concept of

Limbo should not be taught in schools or told to parents who have lost a child before baptism. The notion comes from an incorrect understanding of original sin. The concept of limbo for babies who die without baptism is contrary to my belief in the Lord's love for all children. Children are created to be with God for all eternity in heaven.

Why would a priest refuse to baptize a child because the parents weren't married in the church or aren't active in the parish?

Baptism signifies one's commitment to God. That covenant is lived out in His body, the church, which means practiced in one's local parish. When faced with the decision whether to baptize an infant or not, a pastor has to decide if the parents are going to raise the child Catholic.

Although the parents might not be validly married in the eyes of the church or don't participate in the life of the parish, the pastor could baptize a child if he felt reasonably sure that the parents would raise the child Catholic. Such a decision in favor of baptism would be hard to justify, however, because the child would feel confused by the parents' lack of participation in church life.

This sacrament is not a cold function to be performed to get salvation. Baptism is a commitment of a person, even an infant person, to begin an ever-deepening relationship with Christ. If parents are not willing to follow Christ themselves, then they probably have misunderstood what it means to ask to have a child baptized.

Would an infant who dies without baptism go to

hell? Not if God is the loving person I see in Jesus who died for love of us.

Confirmation and the Holy Spirit

What is the Charismatic Renewal?

The Charismatic Renewal offers an experience of the Holy Spirit similar to that experienced by the apostles in the Upper Room on Pentecost Sunday. With the coming of the Holy Spirit in fire and like a great wind, the apostles' mere acquaintance with Jesus deepened into an intimate knowledge. Timid, guilty people had courage and eloquence to share their love of Jesus with other people, even those who might kill them as they had killed Christ.

When we experience the Holy Spirit through the Charismatic Renewal, we receive a fire and love that helps us to celebrate Mass in a new way. We feel a desire to know about Jesus through reading Scripture and by coming to prayer meetings. We also receive the urge the apostles felt to share the love, forgiveness, and acceptance of Jesus with as many people as possible.

The word *charism* comes from the Greek and means gift. The gift is the Holy Spirit. This gift of the Holy Spirit is not necessarily a brand new coming of the Holy Spirit into a person. Most people in the Charismatic Renewal have already received the Spirit in baptism and confirmation. This coming of the Spirit is a building on the gift of the Spirit already there, a stirring of embers into flames.

This renewal ordinarily happens in a parish during a special time of prayer and study called Life in the Spirit Seminars. Toward the end of these weekly sessions, people are prayed over so that they may receive the "Baptism of the Holy Spirit." Again, this does not take the place of the sacraments of baptism or confirmation but opens hearts to experience the Holy Spirit in a renewed way.

The Charismatic Renewal should not be considered a separate movement in the Catholic Church. Charismatics are called to prudently enrich the whole parish with their experience of the Spirit.

Does the Catholic Church recognize the experience of being "filled with the Holy Spirit"?

Yes. When Jesus ascended into heaven, He promised to be with us until the end of time. He is now with us in a definite way through the power of the Holy Spirit, which helps transform us to manifest the greatness to which He has called us. To be filled with the Holy Spirit is to be filled with the power of Jesus. The Holy Spirit is alive, and He works not only in individuals but in the whole church, as He makes Jesus present through His body.

Being filled with the Holy Spirit gives us power and an understanding about God and life that goes far beyond "earthly" knowledge. The Holy Spirit gives us victory over life's difficulties. Most importantly, being filled with the Holy Spirit gives us a deep personal love for Jesus.

Do Catholics believe in the gifts of the Holy Spirit?

As we read chapter 12 in Paul's first letter to the

Corinthians, we discover that God wants to give us signs of His love—the gifts of the Holy Spirit. One of these gifts, the gift of healing, is the ability to bring wholeness and health where there has been sickness or crippling. The gift of preaching is given so that God's word can be shared. Other gifts are those of teaching, administering, and love (the most important gift of the Holy Spirit). These gifts are presented to us by the Holy Spirit to show us His presence to build up the faith of the community in practical ways. Other gifts of the Spirit for which we as Christians pray are wisdom, fortitude, understanding, counsel, knowledge, piety, and a holy fear of the Lord.

We know we have these gifts by courageously stepping out and exercising them in the service of the community. And so when I see a sick person, I lay hands on him and pray for a healing through the power of the Holy Spirit. I ask the Holy Spirit's help and then stand in front of a group of people and preach of God's love for them. If you wonder if you have a gift of the Holy Spirit, presume you have the gift and use it to reach out to aid others.

What is the gift of tongues?

Speaking in tongues is a gift. Just as two people in love often communicate in a way difficult for others to understand, so in our relationship with God we develop a language that goes beyond logic. It is nevertheless a true expression of our love for our Lord. Another term for speaking in tongues is "using one's prayer language."

If you have the gift of tongues, be prudent about when and where you use it. Paul prayed in tongues in private and reminded the Corinthians that this was not the most important of the gifts. We have to be careful that an individual seeking entrance to the church is not frightened and turned off by the unwise use of the "prayer language." Remember that love is more important than the gift of tongues.

Reconciliation

What is confession?

The sacrament of confession or as it is more correctly called, "reconciliation," occurs when a priest hears a Catholic tell his sins and failings to be cleansed of them.

As we study the early church we find that a person who committed one of four basic sins—adultery, great theft, murder, or idolatry—would go before the bishop and the whole community and confess the sin. After extreme acts of penance, which might involve eating bread and water or wearing sackcloth for long periods, this person was accepted back into the Christian community.

As the Christian community grew in numbers, so did the list of serious sins. It became impossible for individuals to confess in front of the whole assembly and the bishop. Consequently, a priest was appointed by the bishop to take his place as the spokesman of the Lord and the representative of the community.

Don't Catholics go to confession in some dark box?

Today a Catholic can go to the Sacrament of Reconciliation in one of three ways. The first is to go to a confession box, usually in a church. In this form, you don't have to reveal your identity to the priest. You speak behind a grill and tell him your sins. The second way is to sit down with the priest and talk face to face. The third way is to come together with other members of the parish and have a communal confession. In this form you gather in church to praise God, hear of His mercy, reflect on your possible sins, and make a common act of sorrow. Then each person goes privately to a priest and briefly tells his or her sins.

Catholics are free to choose any form of the sacrament. In all three forms the priest speaks words of forgiveness.

Do Catholics go to confession so that they can be free to sin again?

When we Catholics confess, we must have a firm resolve not to commit the sin or sins again. We are supposed to have a real *metanoia*, as the Greeks said, "a change of heart, a willingness to move in a new direction." We must die to self and sin in order to come to life in Christ.

Of course, we know from practical common sense that as long as we are alive, we are subject to temptation and sin. I don't know anyone living who can say, "I am never going to sin again." Despite that practical weakness, a person coming to the sacrament must have a firm resolve, with the help of God's grace, to stay away from sin.

For Catholics, confession is an integral part of spiritual growth. It clarifies the truth with the Lord. If we are unable to share this truth of who we are with other people, then we may be unwilling to grow.

In our mobile, individualistic society, we need to

awaken to the vital importance of the community in our struggle for spiritual maturity. Only by realizing our dependence on others will we ever understand the significance of the Sacrament of Reconciliation.

Why do Catholics have to confess their sins to a man and not directly to God?

When a Catholic commits a sin, the first person to seek forgiveness from is the Lord. Every sin, though, has a bad effect on three relationships: It injures our relationship with *the Lord;* it affects *other people,* even if only slightly; and it harms the *Christian community.*

For example, if I steal $50,000 from you, it isn't enough to ask God's forgiveness. I also must give the $50,000 back to you, as well as make up for any damage you suffered because of my sin. If I had committed this sin as a known Catholic and it became public, I would then tarnish the reputation of the Catholic Church in much the same way a drunken sailor gives a bad impression of the Navy. The church has been commissioned by Christ to act in His name, and the priest speaks in the name of the Lord and of the church community when he offers forgiveness in the sacrament.

Personally I don't like to go to the sacrament of Reconciliation. I confess my sins to one of my closest friends. When I come to him to confess, I have to let down the mask of holiness that I would like others to see. I have to tell him the truth. That is a frightening and humbling risk.

Although I am reluctant to share the truth of my sinfulness and failings, when I confess, there are few joys in life to compare with the love, acceptance, and forgiveness I receive from my confessor, my community, and God. I am empowered to begin again. There is a "born again" experience similar to what Jesus spoke to Nicodemus (John 3:4).

Sin

What can I do about the sin of resentment?

Resentment is a natural human feeling toward someone who has hurt us. The problem with resentment is that when we hold onto it we become enslaved. When we let go of resentment toward others and forgive them, we are free from the brooding suppressed anger which preoccupies our thoughts and actions. If we let go of the resentment and forgive, we are freed to love and build up ourselves and others.

Forgiving another is difficult, especially if our resentment is deep. A few years ago I sponsored a large fund-raising banquet to help pay the bills of my television ministry. A big Hollywood producer ordered two tables and took out two ads in a promotion book. His bill was six thousand dollars. Well, he decided that he didn't want to pay. In anger and frustration I wrote him and called his office. He refused to respond to me for a whole year. I was deeply resentful. Finally, I had to let go of the resentment and forgive him. When I was nursing the resentment, I wasn't free to move ahead with caring for the people in my ministry.

When you find it hard to let go of resentment, think of Jesus on the cross saying, "Father, forgive them, they know not what they do" (Luke 23:34). Break the shackles of resentment and conscientiously love those you resent. Don't allow bad feelings to fester. That's the way to freedom in Christ.

Why do we have temptations?

Temptations are a means of purification. The struggle in temptation calls us to make choices that enable us to become better people.

Frequently, temptation is difficult because it calls on us to choose not between what is clearly good and bad but between what is good and what is apparently good. Because of our desire for pleasure we rationalize. In order to justify a bad choice we highlight the "good" in something that is really wrong for us.

Despite the evil drugs cause his body and the destruction of family relationships, a drug addict chooses them because they offer the seeming good of pleasure and relaxation in a cruel and difficult world.

In my commitment to celibacy, I am often tempted to be unfaithful to that call from the Lord. The temptation is in the form of a caring wife and loving children. Although the wife and children are good, in my heart of hearts I know that the best choice for me is to respond to the Lord's call to celibacy.

Our solace, as we face temptation, is to know that Jesus too faced temptations, struggled with them, and overcame them.

We should not consider temptation a sin. Temptation is a time of honest evaluation. Sin occurs when we choose what we know is wrong.

I don't seem to have the willpower to turn away from a particular sin. What should I do?

Being caught in a web of recurring sin can be most discouraging. If we are human, we know the struggle. When you don't know how to escape, concentrate your efforts on a personal relationship with Jesus. That love relationship will enable you to overcome a sin that has control of you. Remember, the greatest source for overcoming sin is not willpower! Willpower is our human way of trying to conquer a sin that can only be defeated through the power of God.

When we feel depressed or sad because our lives seem to be continually falling into the same pattern of sin and hopelessness, it is beautiful to remember that it was the sinner, Mary Magdalene, and a braggart failure, Peter, whom Jesus loved. Be convinced of Jesus' tender love for you as a sinner. He has a fervent desire never to let go of you.

What should I do about past sins that bother me?

If you remember a past sin and there is a need for reconciliation with some person you have offended, be reconciled! For example, you might have said a harsh word to someone, a word that hurt deeply. You quickly put the incident out of your mind. Several years later, you remember the episode. Write a letter, call, or even better, see the individual in person in an attempt to be reconciled.

As for God's forgiveness, my understanding is that the Lord has forgiven us before we ask forgiveness. Take a few moments and reread the parable of the prodigal son.

I'm having problems with scruples.

When I was younger, I went through seven years of scrupulosity. Scrupulosity is a mental sickness based on a person's inability to trust God. The overscrupulous person sees sin everywhere and can't believe that God has forgiven it. During my years of struggle with scrupulosity, I was unable to understand that God could be loving, understanding, and forgiving. I knew Him only as a God of justice. I was so convinced of my sinfulness and my unworthiness before God that I was sure I was going to hell!

Then God said to me, "I accept you and love you right now for who you are." In this personal love, I was freed to love God because He first loved me. I achieved a better balance in my understanding of God's mercy and justice.

The demands of His love are not obligations to be fulfilled out of fear, rather, my motivation for acting is to please and draw closer to Him who loves me unreservedly.

What is the sin against the Holy Spirit that can never be forgiven?

If a person exercises free will and chooses not to respond to the love of the Holy Spirit, God will not infringe on that freedom of choice. This is the sin against the Holy Spirit. We ourselves choose heaven or hell.

This is not some snap judgment we make; it is the fundamental orientation of our life toward ourselves (hell) or toward God and others (heaven). An impetuous slip of the tongue will not isolate me from a God who loves and understands me completely.

If we are unrepentant, our sin will not be forgiven, but a person always has the chance to seek forgiveness, no matter how terrible the sins. We see this in Jesus' forgiveness of the thief on the cross, the story of the prodigal son, and the story of the laborers who were paid equally even though some worked more hours than others (Matt. 20:12).

Are my sins mortal or venial?

The distinction between mortal and venial sins can be seen in 1 John 5:16–17:

> If anyone sees his brother sinning, if the sin is not deadly, he should pray to God and He will give him life. This is only for those whose sin is not deadly. There is such a thing as deadly sin, about which I do not say that you should pray. All wrongdoing is sin, but there is sin that is not deadly.

The word *mortal* refers to sins which kill a person's relationship with God. The church believes that a person who has committed a mortal sin can be forgiven in the Sacrament of Reconciliation. *Venial* refers to sins that are not deadly. Of course venial sins can have levels of gravity. Physically harming another is more serious than stealing a piece of candy.

Unfortunately, when I was growing up, the notion of "mortal sin" or sin that could send me to hell was used loosely. In those days God was seen as a judge like the Pharisee Jesus rebutted for making law more important than people. There were long lists of possible mortal sins a priest could commit if he didn't follow the rules in celebrating Mass. Eating meat on Friday was a mortal sin. Even some of the quite normal struggles of an adolescent coming to grips with his blossoming sexuality contained the possibility of "easily" committing a mortal sin.

When we speak of sins that jeopardize a person's salvation, we must be very careful not to become judgmental of others. Salvation is a matter between God and the person.

Fortunately, today, there is a much more sane and balanced attitude toward mortal sin. Thomas Aquinas said, "mortal sin is reality but rare." Christ's command to live a high morality is still part of the church's message. The church offers us images of God both as strict judge and as Father of the Prodigal Son. This Father is patient and forgiving beyond logic and beyond our ordinary ways of dealing with wrongdoing.

You mentioned not eating meat on Friday. Has that restriction been changed?

The church has removed the demand for abstinence from meat on Friday, but if this act of self-denial is not observed, another form of penance should be substituted. The option was given because many people were more concerned about fulfilling the letter of the law than fulfilling the spirit of the law. The practice should still be encouraged as a sign of joining the sufferings of Christ as He hung on the cross on Good Friday (Col. 1:24).

I have done many bad things in my life. Can God forgive me?

God doesn't have the problem with forgiveness. We often lack the faith to believe that He is powerful enough to forget the sins we've committed. The Scriptures tell of God the Son's forgiving the woman caught in adultery; of His forgiving His murderers from the cross; of His forgiving Peter, who denied Him. Remember His words: "I did not come to condemn the world but to save the world" (John 12:47).

Why do I feel guilty?

We must be careful not to disregard healthy feelings of guilt because they are often a signal from God that all is not well with our moral life. Guilt can be a sign that we are hurting ourselves and/or others, in addition to hurting our relationship with God.

At other times we should disregard false guilt imposed on our good and wholesome actions. For example, before marriage, a person may have been told about the evils of sexual intercourse, then he or she feels guilty on the wedding night. Since the person has done nothing wrong, such feelings of guilt are unhealthy.

Is doubting God a sin?

Doubting God is not necessarily a sin. Most people struggle with the temptation of doubt. Thomas the apostle doubted the resurrection but moved through the doubt to a beautiful experience of deeper understanding and love of Jesus, "my Lord and my God." Doubt makes us rethink what we might otherwise take for granted. When suffering doubt, we must confront it, then move on and grow. Doubt is the threshold of a stronger commitment to Christ.

We must be careful, though, not to allow indecision to take over our lives. Many people are unwilling to accept the challenge of Jesus' death on the cross. They try to escape this challenge in doubt. It's a safe and secure way to escape being held accountable for our commitment to Christ.

There comes a time, in the midst of doubt, when we have to reach out to Jesus with real faith and commitment and not let go of what He is calling us to do and be.

When you have doubts about your faith, read books on the truth you are doubting. Discuss it with knowledgeable people. Be careful to remain open to what you hear and read while you are doubting.

A newspaper reporter once asked an evangelist friend of mine, "Do you really believe all those things that you're saying? Don't you sometimes doubt?"

"Of course I sometimes doubt," my friend replied, "but I can also doubt the doubt."

Eucharist

Is Jesus really present in the Eucharist?

Catholics believe the words of Scripture, "This is my body . . . this is my blood" (Mark 14:22–23).

Is the Eucharist a symbol? Of course! But every gift, word, and physical expression is a symbol of something deeper. The Eucharist is a symbol and more. The bread and wine become Jesus Christ. This amazes me. When Jesus wants to love, He

136

acts in ways that are greater than our wildest imaginings. What an overwhelming gift! His very self!

Eucharist is a common Catholic word. It means gratitude or thanks. In this sacrament we see the desire of a lover to be with us in that which seems common and vulnerable—a piece of bread and a sip of wine. These signs now, in a way we don't understand, become the reality of Jesus' Body and Blood.

Around the Middle Ages a belief developed that Christ was present in the bread and wine only in a spiritual way. In meetings of Catholic bishops at special councils in 1215 and 1415 and finally at the Council of Trent in 1551, the church defined the change that happens to the bread and wine at Mass to be a complete change into the Body and Blood of Christ. The substances of the bread and the wine are changed. Because of Christ's stark and unequivocal words, they are no longer bread and wine. They are *transubstantiated* into the Body and Blood of Christ.

That's very nice and even inspiring. But don't Catholics get so involved in Holy Communion that they fail to see Christ in others?

As Catholics look at this awesome presence of Christ in the Eucharist, they must be careful not to let it become an end in itself. The reception of communion is a personal experience of the Lord, but it must move us to a deeper commitment to the people with whom we share the Lord. Since food gives energy, we must use the energy to love others, especially those we don't like.

Frequently those who are not Catholic find fault with an understanding of the Eucharist that is too individualistic. Catholics should head off this objection by emphasizing also the community aspects of the Eucharist.

Why do Catholics receive only the bread at Mass while the priest also drinks the wine?

Pastors are urged by church authorities to make the Body and the Blood of Christ more and more available to Catholics who celebrate the Eucharist. Still, Catholics believe our Lord Jesus Christ is truly present, Soul and Divinity, in both the Body and the Blood. Therefore to receive our Lord under just one form or the other doesn't mean we are missing anything. The custom of only the priest receiving the Blood of Christ at the Eucharist dates back to before the 1300s. The reasons the practice developed are varied: risk of spilling the precious Blood, difficulty of preserving the precious Blood after Communion, and the additional time needed for Communion under both forms with large numbers of people.

What about Catholics who are excluded from receiving Communion because of sin?

Often I go through long periods of time when I struggle with knowing if a way of acting is a sin. I justify my actions by recourse to Scripture and by following the example of other "Christians." I pray. I ask the opinions of others. I wrestle with the pros and cons of my actions. During this time of honest

138

struggle, I should receive the Lord as often as possible in Communion.

After this time of speculation, which can last a few seconds or a few years, clarity often comes as to what I should be doing as a Christian. I must leave my state of indecision and choose. If what I choose is contrary to any of the major teachings of Jesus as I see them in my conscience, I would not be honest if I continued to receive in communion a Christ I have rejected in my life.

If I still hunger for Christ in Communion despite my decision not to follow Him, then the deprivation may serve as a force to call me back to His community and teachings.

I am divorced, but I want to receive the sacraments. What should I do?

Catholics are not excluded from the sacraments because they are civilly divorced. The problem arises when they remarry. Jesus prohibited married people from remarrying. If you are divorced and remarried, go to a knowledgeable and sympathetic priest and tell him of your situation. It may be possible for the church to annul your first marriage; that means there may have been a defect in the marriage from the beginning that made the marriage invalid from a sacramental point of view. (For specific information about this see pages 149–150 and my answer to the question "Do you believe in divorce?") Even a several years' marriage with children can be annulled.

If your first marriage cannot be annulled, it isn't the end of the road. If you still believe in your conscience that what you are doing is correct, then you should discuss the matter with a wise priest in the sacrament of reconciliation to see if there is a way for you to receive the sacraments.

Family and Marriage

My marriage is on the rocks. How can I bring new life into it?

I wish I had a nickel for every time I've been asked that question. For me, the key to a successful marriage is a simple one. If you do what I suggest for a few moments each day your marriage will start moving in a much more positive direction.

What is that? Pray for just a few moments each day. Sincerely turn to the Lord in prayer.

Now you might think that I need to come down from my ivory tower as a priest and get realistic. Please hear me. If for a few moments, perhaps only five seconds a day, you will hold each other and pray, God will bless your marriage in a profound way.

Does my five-second plan seem too simple? Believe me, such vulnerability before the Lord and each other is terribly difficult. If you think I make sense and want to try it, you will find that over the long haul, you will come up with excuses for not being able to hold each other and pray for even five seconds a day.

Both aspects of the five-second plan are important. Physical contact whether holding hands or embracing brings a level of serious attention. The honest prayer before God expresses a vulnerability that the Lord blesses with a deepening of a couple's love.

These moments of prayer become the springboard for building up the marriage. Communication and sensitivity to one another improve. If you've tried everything and your relationship is still in a shambles, why not give my five-second plan a try?

Is it wrong not to want children in our marriage?

The fear of having children seems to be increasing. For many the thought of caring for a child is frightening. There is great expense. Then there is the time commitment. Children are so demanding. If a married person wants to have a professional career, a child can make the necessary involvement in work next to impossible. Children are considerd a cause of wrinkles and gray hair. In our age when we aspire to be like the perennially attractive young woman or the exciting, young, party-loving man in television commercials, children seem to be a hindrance.

A teenager's rebellion and anger alone cause so much disruption that one takes pause before choosing to have children.

Yet one of the main ingredients of being a Christian is to give oneself to another person. I have found that paradoxically when I follow Christ and give myself to the needs of others, I have great peace and joy. I believe that when a couple chooses to have a child and picks up the demanding responsibility, the heartache, the letting go of personal dreams for the sake of the child, and the gray hair, Jesus gives them a rich portion of joy and peace.

Why is it so difficult to be married in the Catholic Church?

Many people who were baptized in the Catholic Church no longer celebrate Mass regularly, except perhaps at Christmas and Easter. These same people become indignant when I tell them I won't witness their wedding ceremony. Often I sense that their reason for wanting to be married in a church ceremony is a remote fear of God or a desire to please their parents.

Marriage in the church involves a serious three-way mutual commitment of the couple, the parish, and God. A priest is responsible as the Lord's representative in the parish community to discern if the couple proposing marriage will live up to its commitments. Priests know from experience that too many marriages that started out in seemingly deep love ended in divorce for various reasons.

In most parishes a couple must present themselves to the parish priest six months before the wedding date. They must provide written verification of their baptism. The priest talks with the couple together and separately. Often psychological tests are given to determine strengths and weaknesses of compatibility. They must attend, with other engaged couples, a full day of talks given by marriage experts. An option to this day-long session is to attend a weekend Engaged Encounter. This has many of the same expert talks as the one-day session, but the "engaged encounter" affords a couple a greater chance for dialogue.

When couples come to me to be married, I want to help them clarify their commitment and grow in love.

142

What do Catholics think about wives being submissive?

I admit that I feel uncomfortable whenever I hear Paul's words, "Wives should be submissive to their husbands" (Eph. 5:22). The word *submission* can imply an unhealthy surrender of rights, dignity, and talent. I imagine a wife walking one step behind her husband. The word evokes nothing but indignation and contempt from most of the women I know.

I don't think Paul is advocating this kind of slavery. If we take time to read what comes after the verse in which Paul calls wives to be submissive, we find a more wholesome and balanced understanding of a couple's relationship: "Husbands, love your wives, even as Christ loved the church and handed himself over for her to sanctify her, cleaning her by the bath of water with the word, that he might present himself the church in splendor, without spot or wrinkle or any such thing, that she might be holy and without blemish. So also husbands should love their wives as their own bodies. He who loves his wife loves himself" (Eph. 5:25–28). These words seem different from the image of cold submission of a wife to her husband.

If a husband loves his wife as Paul requests, then he will be sensitive to her. He will not dominate but consult and listen. Christian marriages should be based on open and respectful dialogue between husband and wife. Unity in marriage is not had by bullying domination and control. Concessions and compromise are important ingredients of a growing marriage.

The Christian concept of submission is best seen in Christ's submission to His Father's will.

This submission did not stifle Christ but rather enabled Him to love the Father and lovingly care for the needs of others. This subordination of Christ is seen in Paul's call for husbands and wives to be subordinate *to each other* (Eph. 5:21).

Since Jesus says to "turn the other cheek," should I stay with a husband who abuses me and my children?

I'll never forget the woman who asked me that question. She was gently persistent: "Father, when you get a chance I need to speak with you." She looked to be in her mid-fifties. She was tall and neatly, if simply, dressed.

At the time I was conducting a weekend workshop in Washington State. Because of a hectic schedule, individual counseling was difficult. But in response to her urgent requests, I made time to sit down with her in the auditorium after my last talk on Sunday.

"Father Mike, I have eight children. My youngest is fifteen. Recently I left my husband. I am now living with one of my children in this university town. I'm taking courses that I've always wanted to."

"Why did you leave your husband?" I asked.

"He has never respected me," she responded as her eyes moistened. As I delicately probed more deeply, I found that "never respected me" meant that twice a year He had physically abused her. "I know that I'm supposed to stay with my husband because we were married in the church. But for now I need to get away from him. Is that all right, Father?"

I assured her, "The bond of marriage doesn't in-

144

clude a husband's right to abuse his wife physically.

"But I was raised to believe that Jesus taught us to turn the other cheek."

My stomach turned. In my own life and in the lives of those I love, Christ's words of apparent submission to violence had been the source of so much violence in marriages, of the lack of discipline of children, of the failure to curb social injustices and prevent wars.

As I listened to the woman's tale of woe, I learned that her fifteen-year-old daughter was now imitating her father's violence. "Two weeks ago my daughter beat me up. She hit me in the eye and the jaw. And then when I was down, she kicked me in the stomach. The most disturbing thing was that my husband walked through the room while I was on the floor and didn't help me. He said something about my asking for what I got." Then the woman asked me, "Father, should I go back to my husband and my daughter?"

My stomach turned again. I was repulsed that the words of Jesus could be twisted to play a part in continuing the physical, emotional, and spiritual nightmare she was going through.

"Jesus does not require that you return to your husband to be physically abused," I told this woman. "And as for your daughter, you might ask her to come back, but if she ever lays a hand on you again, my suggestion is that you knock her teeth out."

Her eyes widened in surprise and then filled with tears. She took hold of my arm, gently laid her head on my shoulder, and sobbed.

I later regretted advising the mother to react so violently if her child attempted to hurt her again.

145

But in that moment I was incensed at the savage action of the daughter and the twisted interpretation of Christ's words.

Jesus' advice to turn the other cheek must be seen in context. There is a time for not answering violence with violence. The vengeful retaliation practiced by opposing factions in Lebanon, El Salvadore, or Northern Ireland results in the death of innocent people. There is a time for forgiveness and reconciliation—for turning the other cheek. If we deny Christ's wisdom, the bloodshed seems never to end. The words of Jesus don't mean that we demand the elimination of prisons that protect society from dangerous people. Nor do His words mean that we refrain from verbally and sometimes even physically correcting children when they behave badly. The fifteen-year-old who beat up her mother needs, in my opinion, a good dose of loving physical discipline to bring her to her senses. In much the same way as with the teenager, I believe a nation has a right to defend itself in the face of aggression. God bless the police, disciplining parents, and soldiers when they foster peace and justice!

When Jesus tells us to turn the other cheek, He doesn't mean we should let people walk all over us. Jesus called the scribes and Pharisees hypocrites. Paul refused to be manhandled by his Jewish accusers and appealed to Rome for judgment.

The reality of God's love for me in Christ demands that I love others as I love myself. If I allow people to treat me disrespectfully and use me as an object, I am not being a good Christian. If I fear confrontation or cannot take the risk of rejection, the caliber of my love for others is never going to be worth very much. A Christian must demand respect and dignity from others to be able to give meaningful love to others. Turning the other cheek does not mean that Christians become doormats.

I am afraid to discipline my children. What do you suggest?

Discipline is difficult for an insecure world to accept, and yet family discipline is important. Anger and caring enough to discipline are vital aspects of what it means to be Christian.

We sometimes think of Jesus as a "goody-goody," a man who never said "no," never got angry, never disciplined anyone. And so confrontation in a family is considered unchristian.

We must reexamine Jesus' sense of discipline. He confronted Peter, called him Satan, and told him to get behind Him; He turned over the tables of the money changers; and He expressed His anger at the scribes and Pharisees for their lack of justice and love.

Perhaps we are afraid to exercise discipline on our children because we fear rejection. Don't allow this fear to keep you from speaking the truth to your children.

Sometimes we say we don't discipline our children because we love them so much. In reality we may be shunning discipline because our love is selfish.

Is it possible to have a happy marriage if the spouses belong to different religious denominations?

Most definitely a "mixed" marriage can be a happy one. Still, couples who are planning such a marriage should be made aware of the serious struggles that lie ahead. They must pray much to strengthen their love when tension arises over their different ways of worshiping and understanding God. Jesus is the center of all our love and union. If a couple cannot unite in prayer, private as well as communal, they are going to miss one of the integral parts of love. I strongly recommend premarriage counseling for couples who intend to enter a "mixed" marriage.

Should a couple marry because the woman is pregnant?

A pregnancy outside of marriage doesn't necessarily mean a couple should marry. If the motive for marrying is to escape embarrassment or to give the child a family, those motives are not sufficient. Marriage should be entered into in complete freedom. When difficulties come in a marriage, as they inevitably do, it is too easy for a wife to leave the marriage if she can say, "I married because I was afraid my parents would have rejected me if they had known I was pregnant," or for the husband to leave if he says, "I really didn't love you. I married you because I wanted to be responsible for the baby."

In a world where divorce is so common, I refuse to marry before I live with my boyfriend.

With the high number of divorces and unhappy marriages, I can understand how a couple might consider a trial marriage before they make a commitment. The problem is that a trial marriage's lack of stability fosters insecurity and false expectations.

148

I don't think a man and a woman should live together in a sexual relationship outside of a marriage commitment. Intercourse is more than a commitment of friendship or temporary love. Intercourse, to my way of thinking, implies a commitment of undying love that involves openness to the generation of children. When children come, they need a lifelong commitment from their parents.

I am in favor of an engagement that gives time for serious dialogue and prayer. Psychological evaluation can help the couple identify potential difficulties in their relationship. There are simple tests that take an hour or two to complete and then interpret.

After the couple, their families, and the parish have had a chance to discern the viability of the marriage, a couple should turn to God in great faith and in the hope that He will not let them down. They should commit themselves to marriage for better and for worse.

On a simply human level, marriage, even with the greatest preparation, is a risk. After prudent discernment, a Christian is called to trust that God will bless the union and give each partner the strength to make the marriage successful and enduring.

Do Catholics believe in divorce and remarriage?

Catholics hear Jesus being very strong in His condemnation of divorce. He says that a divorced person who marries another is committing adultery. In Matthew 5:31–32 Jesus says, "It was also said, 'Whoever divorces his wife must give her a

149

bill of divorce.' But I say to you, whoever divorces his wife (*unless the marriage is unlawful*) causes her to commit adultery, and whoever marries a divorced woman commits adultery."

Catholics interpret the phrase "unless the marriage is unlawful" very conservatively. Unlike other denominations Catholics don't see this as a watering down of Christ's clear statement against divorce.

The phrase "unless the marriage is unlawful" refers to the violation of Mosaic Law forbidding marriage between persons of certain blood and/or legal relationships (Lev. 18:6—18). Marriage of that sort was regarded as incest (*porneia*).

In the light of Christ's strong words against divorce the church allows married people to remarry only if the marriage can be determined to be invalid from the beginning and can be annulled.

Some of the factors that pertain to an annulment are:

- Intoxication at the time of the wedding ceremony
- Sexual impotence
- Basic or gross immaturity
- Homosexuality
- Lack of commitment to a lifelong, loving conjugal union
- Force and fear
- Entering the marriage on condition that the partner fulfills certain conditions
- Concealment of some grave situation or personality problem.
- Entering a marriage without an intention of making a permanent union
- Not intending to remain faithful

• One or both parties not wanting to have children

If a couple wants to have their union annulled, they should contact a knowledgeable priest. He will discuss the situation with them and if an annulment is possible will give them the necessary paper work to do. They will answer many questions about the marriage. Witnesses to the marriage are also consulted.

One person can seek an annulment without the support or cooperation of the other marriage partner though the latter is informed that the annulment process has been initiated.

This information is presented to a court called a marriage tribunal. This group of caring people is entrusted by the church with the responsibility of preserving Christ's directions about marriage and divorce. If it decides that there was an invalidating factor, the union can be annulled, and the man and woman are free to remarry.

What should I do when my older children won't go to Mass?

When I was a teenager, I wouldn't have thought of not going to Mass. To miss Mass would be a sin serious enough to get me sent to hell. Unfortunately, this strong discipline often made going to Mass an obligation to be fulfilled rather than a freely chosen act of love for God.

An adolescent naturally revolts against obligations that don't have meaning nor make sense. I explain to teenagers that every Catholic should attend Mass at least once a week. Without this formal community expression of our commitment to the Lord, our love for Him can easily weaken. We

151

may not feel like regularly celebrating our love with the Lord. At times we must move beyond feelings and act on a regular basis because regularity is a key to keeping love alive. Love calls us beyond feelings.

Teenagers know how important dating is. They can spend a great deal of time talking on the phone or in private, but if they don't regularly go to a movie or dinner in public, the love begins to lose its force. Going to church each Sunday is a similar public expression of our love for the Lord.

Try to reach the balance with your children. Clarify the obligation along with the need to foster a free response of love. And if you have tried your best to reach the balance and the children still refuse to go to Mass, don't carry a burden of guilt.

How can I go to Mass if I have young children?

As a general rule, children should be made to feel a part of the church community as soon as possible. The difficulty arises when the children are at an unmanageable age or are not properly disciplined. When people at Mass are more concerned with what a youngster is going to say or do next, they are missing the chance to worship well.

When children cause undue disruption at Mass, I think a "cry room" should be used. But, far better than a cry room would be a class where children could be taught the Scripture lesson of the day at a level they can appreciate. I am pleased that more and more Catholic churches are using this method of caring for small children at Mass.

How can we keep our family together?

It is important for the entire family to pray together every day. Also children and parents need to share their feelings, doubts, and needs before the Lord. Just as a marriage works only when the spouses honestly struggle with one another's problems, so also a family should work together, especially in prayer.

Parents should nightly bless their children by tracing the sign of the cross on their foreheads. This is a visible expression of a parent's warm acceptance of children even after having disciplined them during the day.

Do I sound like I am coming from another planet? I can hear you muttering, "This is about the most impractical thing I have ever heard." I know that getting a family together each day seems an impossibility. Perhaps to do it each day *is* impractical. Still, I don't think it is impossible for a family to pray regularly. It all comes down to a question of priorities. In my life I have to struggle with developing daily habits of community prayer, or my good intentions go out the window.

If a family is small and growing, daily prayer can happen more easily than when the children have grown. Even in this later stage, the family can pray together regularly.

The best time, the style of prayer, and the duration of prayer need to fit each family: in the morning, at a meal, in the evening? The prayer can be a reading of Scripture, an Our Father, or a spontaneous prayer. It can last five seconds or longer. The key is making sure that it happens on a regular basis.

Leadership in the Church

Who is the pope to Catholics?

Catholic Christians believe the pope is the true successor of St. Peter. Just as Jesus gave Peter the keys to the Kingdom of heaven (Matt. 16:16–19), so these keys have been passed down to more than 260 Popes for nearly two thousand years. The keys represent God's authority; their possession thus identifies the man to whom God has given authority.

Toward the end of his life, Peter came to the center of the Roman world. He became the first leader of the church of Rome. The present day pope is the successor of Peter. As we learn from church history, the bishop of Rome was considered the primary bishop of the Christian world. The bishop of Rome was looked to for the final word on any major question about the revelation of Jesus.

Is the pope infallible?

If we admit that Christ has given to His church the responsibility of maintaining and clarifying His revelation in an infallible way, it follows naturally that its spokesman must likewise be infallible. If Peter and his successors could teach false doctrine, they would cease to be the rock foundation on which the church is built. The gates of hell would prevail against it, which is contrary to our Lord's promise. The faith of the brethren would not be strengthened, and Jesus' flock would not be fed with the true food of divine faith (Matt. 6:18–19, Luke 22:31–32).

The pope is infallible, the church believes, only on certain occasions when he speaks *ex cathedra* ("from the chair" which means the chair of authority of Peter the Apostle); thus he is speaking officially as supreme pastor of the universal church and is intending to define a doctrine regarding faith and morals as being revealed. The intention of speaking infallibly must be clearly expressed.

Does everything that the pope teaches carry the same weight of authority?

The Second Vatican Council said, no. There are levels of teaching authority. Some are more binding than others. In the council's decree on ecumenism, No. 11, the bishops taught, "In Catholic teaching there exists an order or hierarchy of truths which vary in their relationship to the foundations of Christian faith." When the pope joins the bishops from around the world and pronounces that Jesus is both God and man, Catholics see that as a definite clarification of the revelation of Jesus. The doctrine of Jesus' divinity is far more central to Christian faith than a statement on the teachings of Galileo.

When the pope talks about science his opinion is not infallible. Most scientists' opinions would be more trustworthy. When the pope makes laws, he is legislating rather than teaching. When the pope teaches religion his opinion must be respected. When the pope makes it clear that he is teaching infallibly, that statement is infallible.

Popes have made clearly infallible statements only twice in the last one-hundred and forty years: once in the doctrine of the Immaculate Conception, which says that Mary was assumed soul and body into heaven.

When a person faces this difficult question

about following a papal teaching on a not infallible matter, a faithful sense of openness to the pope's teaching as a source of Christian unity is necessary.

Even if a person might have a lifelong struggle with papal teachings, there should be an underlying respect and desire for unity. Despite all the weaknesses and failures of popes in the past, Catholics look to these leaders as sources of unity when conflicting opinions about Jesus' revelation are proposed. Whenever the pope speaks, I am attentive. God has given him an office of authority that can not be taken lightly.

As an intellegent person who has read history, I know that popes have made statements that have proved to be wrong. There were papal policies that I would not endorse were they given today. For example I disagree with the pope's having temporal and military power in the time of the papal states in Italy. Three papal pronouncements over a seventeen-year period (1569–1586) had unequivocally denounced and condemned usury—the lending of money at interest. The condemnation of Galileo was shortsighted and foolish. Although I don't endorse these statements, I can still adhere to the pope's ability to teach infallibly when questions arise about revelation.

History has shown that popes haven't always been correct.

If I can bring this seemingly complex problem a bit closer to home, there is a need of authority in any family. Today we stress more of a shared authority of husband, wife, and children. But there is a bottom line. When there isn't a consensus, ei-

156

ther everyone remains in confusion or we concede authority to someone who breaks the deadlock. In my family my father was usually the one who made the ultimate decision about moving to another town. Dad also made decisions on what we would do on a weekend, and he gave permission to my brother-in-law to marry my sister. Although he maintained his authority, different decisions carried different weight. Some decisions were more important than others. Though I might have disagreed strongly with my dad, I didn't want to change my family name. I wanted a bond with him and the rest of the family. This image helps me understand the authority of Peter as we see it in the pope.

Clarity about what is infallible and what's not is important. On a simple level, though, I need to believe in the authority of the pope and unite with him to maintain the church's universal unity. Of course, he will say some things about which I disagree. With prudence, so as not to scandalize and confuse others, I can question certain teachings. Catholics are never asked to give a blind assent that doesn't allow a search for meaning. Still, through all the doubts and struggles, I want to maintain the unity of the Catholic community.

I read that a high percentage of Catholics don't follow the pope's teaching on birth control.

The struggle for most Catholics comes when the teaching of the pope is in conflict with a personal moral decision. Although all the recent popes have condemned artificial birth control, sociological surveys of Catholics show that high percentages

157

practice the condemned action because their consciences justify them in so doing. Some Catholics agree that papal teaching on birth control is infallible.

As a priest giving direction on birth control, I make a point of clarifying what the church teaches. I don't believe in using threats and impersonal pat answers to bully people into doing what the church wants. I listen and then try to explain the positive reasons why the church takes the stands it does. As long as there is no negative reaction that would cause public scandal to the church teaching, I am willing to show some of the Lord's patience. I also want to respect the person's freedom of conscience and relationship with God. I will discuss later the church's teaching on birth control.

If popes made mistakes about the Inquisition, if Pope Alexander VI had illegitimate children, how can you put such faith in these sinful human leaders?

Although I believe the pope is infallible in matters about the direct revelation of Jesus, I also acknowledge him as a human being like me.

I reconcile this seeming dilemma by looking at St. Peter. Peter, the first pope, was not a perfect man. Christ cared for him and asked him to assume the role of leadership despite Peter's great weaknesses. At one point Peter denied the reality of the coming death of Jesus and our Lord had to respond, "Get behind me, Satan" (Mark 9:23). Then when Christ had been taken prisoner, Peter denied he knew Jesus (Mark 14:71). In Galatians 2:11 we find that Paul had to confront Peter over

158

his attitude toward uncircumcised Gentiles. Despite these failings, the church turned to Peter as its leader in keeping it faithful to the revelation of Jesus.

Despite all these papal failures, do you still want to hold onto the papacy?

You have such a negative attitude toward the men who have been popes. A look through history will show that the vast majority of them were Holy-Spirit-filled men who were an honor to the leadership role they had. Balance your rightful concerns about the morals of certain popes with equally valid appreciation for the overwhelming number who were saintly, courageous men.

As a Catholic I look to this bishop of Rome as the leader Christ has chosen to maintain unity among His followers and faithfulness to the revelations of Jesus.

Through the centuries millions of people have had a problem with the idea of the pope continuing the role of Peter. Why don't you join the reformers?

A quick look at history shows that the authority of the pope has been a source of tension to various followers of Jesus at various times. The Reformation came about because many lacked confidence in the pope's authority over the revelation of Jesus. I am not inclined to join the reformers and move away from the line of authority passed on by the Holy Spirit to the Catholic Church. I see the proliferation of independent Christian churches founded by well-intentioned people as a problem of even greater magnitude than the struggle with the pope's authority. The move away from unity causes non-Christians not to be attracted to Jesus because of the prejudice and antagonism among His followers.

I strongly feel that Christianity must have greater unity based on unity with the human authority (the pope) encouraged by Jesus. I want to look to the office of Peter as established by Christ to preserve that unity today.

We do need the inheritors of Peter's leadership to keep us in line with the revelation of Jesus as it is inevitably questioned down the ages.

Why are there so many levels of membership in the Catholic Church: pope, bishops, monsignors, priests, deacons, and then, the bottom of the rung, the laity? Aren't we all called to be one in Christ?

The division of authority comes from Christ's basic endorsement of a hierarchy. While Christ was living on the earth, He chose apostles and gave a special prominence to Peter. He chose seventy-two disciples distinct from the people to whom they ministered. In the early church further distinctions evolved because of the needs of the communities: deacons, elders, bishops, and presbyters. The role of the present-day priest is an evolution of these various ministries.

The danger to Christ's call for a hierarchy is that some people can start thinking they are more important than they are. They can start "lording it over" others. Christ knew of that danger and repeatedly demanded in His teaching that a leader was one who became the servant of others. His

160

strongest teaching on that came at the Last Supper when he knelt and washed the feet of His disciples. Church law today says that all the faithful enjoy a radical equality.

I personally struggle with hierarchical differences of dress. Many prefer clerics and members of religious orders to dress differently from the way lay people dress. They see the different clothes as a sign of dedication to God. I agree that clothes can be a challenge to come closer to God for those who see such clothes worn. I can support and respect that stand.

Unfortunately, in my experience, a collar, a cassock, or religious garb frequently becomes a symbol of superiority and of being special rather than an imitation of Christ's common and unassuming way of dressing.

I heard that some archbishop left the church with many of his followers. Would you tell me about that?

One of the greatest scandals of Christianity is the fact that there are some 22,800 different groups of believers. This is discouraging in light of Jesus' prayer just before He died: "I pray . . . . that they may all be one as you, Father, are in me and I in you" (John 17:20–21).

No sooner had Christ entrusted the direction of His church to His followers than the church started to fragment. We live today with the glaring separations between Rome and the Greek Orthodox Church and Rome and the protestant churches.

When we look at people who have led such separations, we find a common denominator among

161

them. Each person did so because he believed that he was doing what God wanted. He felt that he was following the direction God had chosen for His church.

A church separation, like a divorce from marriage, can involve feelings of guilt, fear, and great pain. Any normal person dislikes separation, but if our conscience tells us we must act a certain way, we must respond to that call. A person is finally accountable to God. Often personal decisions can have devastating effects on others. This can be seen in a divorce or a schism from a mother church. Often we wish that there had been more patience, dialogue, and perhaps concessions.

Catholics were greatly saddened by the decision of the French Archbishop Marcel Lefebvre to leave the church. When he consecrated four bishops without permission from Rome, he ended a twenty-year struggle to reconcile his beliefs with the Vatican's.

During and after the Second Vatican Council in 1965, Archbishop Marcel Lefebvre disagreed with some of the decisions of the council and the changes that came into the church. He wanted to hold onto Latin in the Mass as it had been for centuries because, he argued, the new liturgy did away with awe and mystery.

Statements about religious freedom were, Archbishop Lefebvre believed, contrary to former church teachings. He was concerned with the ecumenical movement. The new respect of protestants bothered him. To his chagrin, the Church of Rome even went so far as to say that the Holy Spirit could be alive in people who had formally been considered heretics. Yet the changes the council initiated were not violations of the revelation of Jesus, which is the basis of judging whether a tradition can be changed.

Through the years, Lefebvre began to form a group of followers who celebrated Mass the way it was celebrated before the Second Vatican Council. In his own seminaries he began ordaining priests in his fraternity of St. Pius X to insure the continuation of things the way they used to be.

The Vatican bent over backwards to forestall a separation. Strong concessions were made to Archbishop Lefebvre. The Vatican was aware that the liturgical changes of the 1960s were often introduced very quickly. Many people didn't receive proper instruction about them. Many were alienated. The Vatican gave Catholics the right to celebrate Mass in Latin under certain circumstances. The Vatican was willing to allow Lefebvre to ordain a bishop to continue to give leadership to his fraternity as long as Rome had the right to choose the bishop.

Finally the archbishop was not satisfied with Rome's concessions. He went against the rules of the church and ordained four bishops of his own choosing. We might compare this act to a vice president of General Motors deciding to hire four vice presidents to make a new car when the board of directors told him that he couldn't do so. The chairman of the board of directors would have to say that the disobedient vice president was no longer a member of General Motors.

The break by the archbishop was certainly conclusive, but the Vatican is mounting vigorous efforts to bring about reconciliation so that Christ's desire for unity among Christians can be fostered. Although the archbishop decided to leave, the church will do all it can to welcome him back.

I pray that Archbishop Lefebvre and his followers will not be so obsessed with the good they stand for that they ignore the harm they cause by their separation.

Why are priests called "Father"?

I marvel at many protestants who greet me with the title "Father." They do so very much against their principles but out of a loving desire not to cause further division. In the backs of their minds, I think they are confounded as to how a Christian could take on such a title in direct violation of Christ's words. Let me explain.

In His life as a servant, Jesus gave us an example of how to be leaders. At the Last Supper, He got down and washed the feet of His apostles. He was opposed to any leader assuming a haughty or superior attitude. Right in line with His actions and His teachings, He told us in Matthew 23:2–10 not to call anyone "Father," "Rabbi," or "Teacher."

I think one would do an injustice to Christ to think He was opposed to calling the father of five children a "father" or the leader of a synagogue a "rabbi" or the young woman who is instructing thirty-five first graders a "teacher." Jesus is not opposed to using words to describe what a person is doing.

Christ is opposed to titles that persons use to "Lord it over" (Luke 22:25) others. If a person uses a title to be exempted from service of others or to feel better than others, the titles should not be used.

164

As a priest who uses the title "Father" before my name, I must listen closely to Christ's words. Am I using the title to consider myself better than others? If so, I should not use it.

For me, the title "Father" is closely connected to the vow I have taken to live a life of celibacy. I have chosen not to marry a woman and generate children. That denial for the kingdom of God of what is very natural doesn't eliminate my responsibility to be a father. I must use my love and creativity to serve the needs of others to whom I am committed through the church.

When people call me "Father" they challenge me and remind me to love the people of the kingdom and not shirk my responsibilities of fatherhood.

St. Paul was a celibate. He wrote of his spiritual fatherhood in his letter to the slave owner Philemon about the slave Onesimus, "I urge you on behalf of my child Onesimus, whose father I have become in my imprisonment" (Phil. 10). He writes to the Corinthians, "Even if you should have countless guides to Christ, yet you do not have many fathers, for I became your father in Christ Jesus through the gospel" (1 Cor. 4:15).

And if you ever find me using the title "Father" to imply I'm better than you or if I am not loving you in service, call me Mike.

Recently I've heard about some Catholic priests going to jail for molesting children or getting girls pregnant. What's going on?

In recent years the media has exposed the crimes of some Catholic priests. For example, a few years ago seven priests in Los Angeles were said to have had sexual relations with one woman. The other night a network newscast told of the indictment of a priest who was charged with over thirty counts of sexual abuse of young boys.

As a priest, I am saddened by these cases and I can understand the anger of people who feel they have had their esteem for these priests dashed.

I value the Catholic priesthood. I don't like to see my ideal of it tarnished. I have the unrealistic wish that priests will never do wrong.

A Catholic priest is a man trying to respond to a very serious call to follow Jesus. He is chosen by God, through the church community, to be a special leader in prayer and the sacraments. A priest is set aside, in the hearts of most of the faithful, to be a person who has a close relationship with God.

The vows of a priest often run prophetically counter to many values that society incorrectly holds to be acceptable. Celibacy speaks of a love that is opposed to the distorted values regarding love and sex advocated in so many movies, magazines, records, and TV shows.

Some priests take the vow of poverty, which implies a life-style that seems a far cry from media advertising that promises security and meaning in life to those who amass material possessions. "At death, the one with the most toys wins," as the bumper sticker says.

A priest's obedience to a bishop's difficult order catches our attention when we find ourselves enmeshed in an overly selfish understanding of freedom. The prophetic call of the priesthood speaks of an ideal. It is an attempt to imitate Christ in a radical way. Still, scandals do arise. They have been present throughout the history of the church. But they cause us to feel letdown.

Although I aspire to the ideals of the priesthood, I know that I am human. I am a sinner. Being a religious leader makes me no less vulnerable to the seductions of evil than any other person inside or outside the church.

Jesus' strongest words of anger were directed not to the struggling people but mainly to the religious leaders, the scribes and Pharisees: "You hypocrites!" (Matt. 15:7). Jesus spent a great deal of time training and challenging his leaders to be people of service. We who are leaders have a big responsibility to carry on that service.

In His parable about the tax collector and the Pharisee, Jesus tells a story about how easily a religious leader can fail in the service to God. The Pharisee was a prominent religious leader. In the parable the Pharisee prayed, "I thank you, God, that I am not greedy, dishonest, or immoral, like everybody else. I thank you that I am not like that tax collector."

The tax collector stood at a distance and would not even raise his face to heaven, but beat on his breast and said, "God, have pity on me, a sinner!" And Jesus says that the tax collector, not the haughty religious leader, was in the right with God when he went home.

Christ's message in this parable of the repentant sinner, coupled with the scandal caused by some of my fellow priests, calls me to humility and to forgiveness.

May I ask you to forgive us priests when we go wrong. Demand redress for the evil we have caused. But above all, when we strive to be the prophets God has called us to be, give us your love.

What should I do when hurt by a priest who spoke rudely to me?

Priests are human. We make mistakes. But we must, at all times, keep our eyes on Jesus who assures us of unfailing love. When a priest hurts you, don't let the hurt fill you with resentment. Don't be defensive; take the initiative. Shower him with love through words and actions of concern, patience, support, and love. You'll scare him to death and free yourself and him!

Women

Women don't have much voice in church decisions, do they?

I am deeply concerned about the place of women in the church today and in the past. The all-male leadership of the church is in drastic need of re-evaluation. I am happy to say that the Catholic bishops in the United States have come out with a draft statement about women that is filled with openness toward them, compassion for them, and even apologies for past discrimination against them. Can you imagine?

The official church leadership is decidedly male. But for several years now, many women in the church have been expressing a growing displeasure at the lack of respect they have been getting. Catholic women have reached a level of education in the United States that is unparalleled in the history of the world. This education has fed an indignation towards many insensitive male clerics who are giving them direction without consultation. "No taxation without representation" was the catalyst of the American revolution. A similar sentiment is expressed by many Catholic women today in a church that often doesn't seem to value their gifts.

Reactions to the male leadership in the church have taken various forms. One nun stood silently before the pope with an extended arm and a clenched fist. In a more mild manner, a mother of seven mustered her courage and asked her conservative pastor if she could be the first woman to help distribute Communion in her parish.

The bishops tried to respond to women's needs with a document that airs much of the positive and negative thinking about women in the church. The document was not put together hastily. The bishops consulted some seventy-five thousand Catholic women for their thoughts and feelings concerning their role in the church.

The letter challenges priests and bishops to eliminate patronizing, condescending attitudes toward women. It says that sexist attitudes or an inability to deal with women as equals should be considered indications that a seminarian is unfit for ordination to the priesthood!

In one of the most powerful sections of the letter, the bishops say that we of the clergy "must and do pledge to reject clearly and consistently human structures and patterns of activity that in any way treat women as of lesser worth than men. . . . We, therefore, regret and confess our individual and collective failures to respond to women as they deserve."

In other sections the bishops call the church to a profound interior renewal to abandon sexist and discriminatory language and attitudes that have denied women opportunities, ignored or trivialized their contributions, and placed unequal burdens on them.

The bishops say the church needs to do more pastorally, not only for married couples but for women who are single, divorced, or widowed, and for the many women trying to raise families as single parents.

Although loud voices are heard asking that women should be ordained priests, this issue is not being considered officially. There is, though, a call for women to participate in all roles in the church short of ordination. That would include serving at the altar during Mass and even the possibility of women being ordained deacons.

The letter, "Partners in the Mystery of Redemption," has opened a window of justice for Catholic women that I hope will never be closed.

Why are Catholic leaders so opposed to women becoming priests?

Officially the Church teaches that the ordination of women priests is contrary to the tradition of Christianity. Jesus chose males for the leadership of His community.

One argument put forth against the ordination of women is that Jesus didn't choose priests who were women, so we must follow His lead. Personally, I find this argument difficult to maintain. If you follow that reasoning to a logical conclusion, then there should be no Gentile priests because Jesus chose only circumcised Jews to be His priests.

Further fuel for controversy was stoked when the Vatican's own official group of Catholic Scripture scholars couldn't find a basis in scripture for denying ordination to women. They found that the first leaders were not "priests" in the sense we use the term today.

There is a healthy struggle going on in the church to understand the meaning of the present discipline of not ordaining women. We must continue to listen to bishops and theologians, especially female theologians, as they wrestle with this question.

I think the biggest obstacle to ordaining women is that for almost two thousand years, it has not been done in the Catholic Church.

Sacrament of the Sick

What is the special ritual that Catholics have for the dying?

The sacrament that the Catholic Church uses today to express Christ's care and healing for the sick and dying is called the Sacrament of the Sick. This is a new name. When I first learned about the sacrament in religion class it was called Extreme Unction or the Last Rites. (Not an exciting image!) The sacrament was given only when a person was in danger of death, and so it had a grim place among the Seven Sacraments.

A few years ago I had a reminder of how much this negative image of the sacrament is still with us, even with younger Catholics. A friend of mine had just had a baby. She gave me a call to come and see her and the little infant. With a smile on my face, I walked out of the elevator on the maternity ward floor. A group of five teenagers was seated opposite me. When they looked up and saw my black suit and collar, one of the youths shattered my happiness with the question, "I wonder who died?"

Today you don't have to be at death's door to receive the Sacrament of the Sick. All people who are seriously ill qualify: someone about to undergo serious surgery or someone suffering from old age. Even children can receive the sacrament provided they are seriously ill, yet mature enough to understand what holy anointing means.

For Christians, illness can be a time for deepening our faith in Jesus. As we review His life in the Gospels, we are strengthened and comforted when we see His tireless care for the sick: the lepers, the blind, the lame, and the deaf. We are not alone. God, our Creator is not indifferent. Jesus is our hope.

As we look closely at what Jesus did, we find that physical healing wasn't His only concern. He always addressed the sickness of sin. Remember the healing miracle that took place when the paralyzed man was lowered through the roof into His presence? There were so many people crowded into the house where Jesus was teaching that they couldn't carry their friend through the front door. Before Jesus healed the man's body, He forgave his sins. He said, "Child, your sins are forgiven" (Mark 2:1–12).

Jesus cares for the whole person. Far more important than the cure of a physical sickness, a cure that might push away the temporary inevitability of death, our spiritual selves are also in need of healing.

Jesus' concern for the suffering was not that of a distant God who swept into the world like a magical fairy godfather, did His good deeds, and then returned to heaven unscathed. No, our God, in Jesus, became wounded for our sakes. He suffered excruciating loneliness, fear, helplessness, brutality, and defeat.

Because of His agonizing fear and dread in the Garden of Gethsemane, God understands our suffering. Through the humiliation and torn flesh of His scourging, God knows of the suffering that we alone seem to bear.

What do Catholics believe about miracles?

I once spoke with a Presbyterian friend of mine about my struggle to understand miracles. He laughed, "The only Christian knowledge I had of miracles was from you Catholics: There were miracles in the town of Lourdes where Mary is supposed to have appeared. Also any time you proclaimed somebody a saint, she had to have so many miracles attributed to her. Come on, you Catholics certainly believe in miracles."

I had to admit he was right. We Catholics believe in miracles.

I went to Scripture, and I found that Jesus entrusted the power to perform miracles to His followers. I couldn't see how that commission stopped with the apostles and the early church. Christ's strong desire to preach the kingdom of God wouldn't end. If He wanted us to continue His work, He would give us the means He used: preaching, teaching, driving out of Satan, mastery over nature, forgiveness of sins, and healing.

Since acknowledging that power I have had the courage to pray for healings. Have I seen changes?

173

Definitely. People with physical sickness have regained their health; spouses in marriages that were "on the rocks" have experienced a deepening in love. People overcome with discouragement and despair have found hope and direction in their lives. Frequently healing happens when I celebrate the Sacrament of the Sick. At other times I simply lay hands on hurting people. At other times I merely talk to the Lord to ask His help for them.

Are my prayers always answered? Not always in the way I request. I have come to believe that God cares deeply for everything that I bring to Him. My prayers make a difference. In His wisdom, He often reacts to my prayers in bigger and grander ways than I can understand. I think of God looking at my requests for healing through a telescope, while I see things with only a microscope.

Is it un-Christian to fear death?

The fear of death is natural, especially since death involves the unknown. We fear those things we haven't experienced. As we understand that our love for Jesus is not just an invention of our imaginations, we can envision death as a glorious transition to a more full and beautiful relationship with Him. Still, here on earth, our knowledge of Him is incomplete. However, we must continually give attention to Jesus' promise of everlasting life—He will never forget or change it. Although we may fear death, we know it is going to be our ultimate victory because of our faith in His promise. We don't know exactly *what* lies beyond the grave, but we know *who* is.

Why do some Catholics have wakes?

A wake is the event when we show our sorrow and sadness for the one who has died and for ourselves because we are without the person we love. It is a natural human reaction to go through this period of grief, wailing, and moaning. Feeling sad and crying are nothing to be ashamed of. These feelings are natural. They are necessary.

After we express our sorrow, we concentrate on the reality of the risen Savior and of His promise of a victorious life. Because we believe our loved ones are in heaven with the Lord, enjoying the fullness of all His promises, we can and should be joyful, even in the face of death.

SECTION 4

Catholic Moral Teaching

The words of Jesus in the Gospels are filled with high expectations. He says that He wants us to be perfect as His heavenly Father is perfect. Now that certainly is an ideal to work for.

We could become indignant until we think of people we know who have lovingly called us to develop our talents. I am thinking of parents, teachers, coaches, and religious leaders. These demanding people in my life loved me. They saw in me more than I saw. In the same spirit as Christ, they called me to perfection.

In the midst of all the loving demands to live an outstanding moral life, we must never forget that the God who demands much also is patient and understanding. He knows us. He has experienced our temptations.

As we evaluate contemporary Catholic morality, you should know that there have been three major shifts in emphasis in the last fifty years on how Catholics decide an action's morality: (1) there has been a shift from obedience to divine law to concern for human and gospel values; (2) when we evaluate a moral act, we need to consider a person's basic commitments, dispositions, and social relations; (3) a Christian is called to strive not only for personal moral perfection but also to meet the needs of others.

Sexual Morality

I see church leaders frequently acting out of frustrated sexual lives and trying to control the sexuality of others. Be married for twenty years. Raise five children and then talk to me about sexuality.

I agree with your objection. As a male celibate my knowledge of sexuality is restricted. What do I have to rely on when I talk about sex? Well, as a human being I am aware of my own sexual drive. I deal with objective facts and personal experience as a person who grew up in a family. I have talked with unmarried, married, and divorced people. I am exposed to the same media distortions of sexuality that you are. I am not completely out of touch with the experience of marriage and relationships.

I study to see if the official Catholic statements on sexuality are in touch with the truth of human nature and the teachings of Jesus. If they are, I want to follow the teachings.

Every now and then some objective celibate who can take an objective view of the subject needs to wave a flag of concern—as Jesus did; He was celibate. I hope that I can speak with a certain detached objective honesty about sexuality. Take what I say along with what people who have more practical experience say.

I get the impression that the church is preoccupied with saying no to sex, especially sexual intercourse.

I too hear a strong concern about and perhaps even a preoccupation on the part of the church on sexual matters and especially sexual intercourse. I wonder if it isn't society that is more concerned with sex while the church is merely reacting to the preoccupation. The church wants sex to be a vital part of a committed marriage.

Personally, although intercourse is not a part of my life, I hold it in high esteem. I see it as the most exalted act of creation two humans can perform. To give oneself to another in sexual intercourse is to make a gift of supreme love that allows two people to be one with each other and God.

When I speak out about restrictions on intercourse, I do so out of a desire to make sure that this sacred act isn't cheapened. The value of sexual intercourse only in marriage must be protected at all costs, and so I will speak out when I think this value is not being respected.

Couples must be wary that with the deep satisfaction and building of love that intercourse brings to their union, this act of love doesn't become a selfish, using, manipulative, and destructive act. Can we ignore the number of divorces, unwanted pregnancies, the resulting single parents, and the abortions?

I think that many fear that the church is trying by moral force to require a puritanical, unhealthy outlook on sex. I don't see that extreme as the church's goal at all. I look to the church's teaching on sexuality for a more balanced, honest look at sexuality's beauty.

Homosexuality

What do Catholics believe about homosexuality?

I got into a rather heated discussion with a homosexual the other day. I said, "Sexual activity between two people of the same sex is wrong."

He responded, "You are very insensitive. I wouldn't want to come to your church."

I certainly didn't want him to stay away from my church because he was struggling with homosexuality. I told him, "My church is a place for people who are struggling to discern what is right and wrong. But my church doesn't consider sexual activity outside of heterosexual marriage to be in line with the teachings of Jesus."

The man then made an impassioned reply: "My attraction to a member of the same sex is a condition I was born with. I don't feel that I would ever be able to be attracted sexually to a woman. If you ignore this fact, you deny me the love and support of Christ and His church. I desperately need that support!"

I said, "Your homosexual *inclinations* do not exclude you from full membership in my church. You just couldn't be sexually active with another man and have the church condone it. That restriction of sexual activity to marriage is the same for a homosexual as it is for a heterosexual.

"Don't you understand?" he pleaded. "I need intimacy like other people. Since I can't have it with women, I've got to have it with men."

"Of course you need intimacy," I said, "but you don't have to achieve that by sexual activity with another person."

"Does a person who is a homosexual have to remain chaste to be a Catholic?" he asked.

I responded affirmatively: "I know that chastity is a difficult way to live. At the same time it is filled with much joy, challenge, and creativity. Almost everyone thinks that sexual intercourse is the only way to express love. Well, chastity can be a wonderful way of expressing love and caring for people even if I don't sleep with them." I waited for a response but it didn't come.

Should we use the mass media to encourage people to use condoms to save our nation from AIDS and unwanted pregnancies?

There has been a great deal of public discussion regarding the presentation of advertising about contraceptives via television. This dialogue has become more intense in light of the former surgeon general's public comments advocating the use of condoms as a preventative against the spread of AIDS.

The Catholic Church is deeply concerned about AIDS victims. This follows the example of Jesus who healed the dreaded disease of leprosy, which evoked fears similar to those caused by AIDS today. Into the lives of those lonely, hopeless people suffering from leprosy, Jesus brought a loving physical touch. He brought healing.

Despite this care for suffering people, most Catholic bishops are opposed to using the mass media to advertise the sale of condoms to curb the AIDS epidemic.

Many of the bishops see this advertising of condoms as the wrong solution to the spread of AIDS. These bishops fear that such advertising would condone the use of sex outside the commitment of marriage. These bishops advocate abstinence from illicit sexual activity as the best solution to curbing the spread of AIDS.

Advertising condoms on television may well teach the young:

- The condom is *the answer* to the spread of AIDS—and other sexual diseases.
- People have no obligation to themselves and others beyond "safe sex."
- People are incapable of sexual responsibility and discipline.

I was recently accused during a radio program of being party to killing people by my opposition to the commercial advertising of condoms. The argument went that since people who have contracted AIDS are going to have illicit sex anyway, to not encourage the use of condoms is to be party to the killing of the people who will contract AIDS.

I believe that people who are acting in an improper way should be challenged to accept the freedom and peace of acting in the proper way. To concede to a sinful way of acting is to belittle a person's potential for choosing the greater good, which in this case, I believe, is abstinence from illicit sexual activity.

I believe in the concept of sound sex education, but that concept goes beyond the teaching of "safe sex." Sexual relations between people committed to love in marriage should be taught as one of the most noble and sacred human actions. This education is both the duty and right of parents. They should be irate that condom advertising is undercutting their place in sex education.

I fear that the commercial encouragement to use condoms will also further complicate the problem of the high number of pregnancies among teenagers who are not prepared for motherhood or marriage. I fear that such ads are likely to confirm the view that sexual activity outside of marriage is to be taken for granted. I refuse to belittle human beings by saying they can profane the sacred act of sex with condoms because "everybody's doing it anyway."

In all our discussion, let's not forget the financial boon television advertising will bring to the condom industry. Recently condom stocks rose eight dollars a share! John Silverman, president of Ansell Americas, the seller of LifeStyles condoms, commented that "AIDS is a 'condom marketer's dream'" (*Time,* Feb. 16, 1987). Gordon O'Reilly, vice president of merchandising at Bartell Drugs, said that condom sales by the chain are at least 50 percent higher than they were two years ago.

The proposed TV campaign is not just a "public service"; it is a commercial undertaking of considerable financial potential, for the manufacturers of contraceptives, the advertising industry, and the media. It seems not unreasonable to suggest that if this were genuinely an educational effort on behalf of the common good, the strategy followed would be a not-for-profit "public service" campaign.

Isn't the scourge of AIDS a punishment from God?

A statement making the rounds in many Christian circles runs something like this: "Those homosexuals are finally getting what they deserve. A person can abuse God's law for only so long. The Lord will eventually catch up with him. AIDS is God's way of bringing back sanity to sexual behavior. AIDS is God's way of wreaking vengeance on sinners."

The AIDS epidemic does seem to be a natural result of people's not following God's direction, and the sickness has awakened a strong need to abstain from illicit sex. Yet there's something foul smelling about the self-righteous judgments contained in the comment above. The image of God is so vengeful; it just doesn't sit well with me.

We Christians must distance ourselves from any judgment about people suffering from AIDS. Statements about their sinfulness or lack of it are not for us to make. When we sit in judgment on a person, we are falling into the same original sin of Adam and Eve in their attempt to be like God. It is not for the Christian to make paternalistic judgments but to be a person of service, forgiveness, and mercy.

As for my struggle with the idea of a vengeful God, I know that you can quote me book and verse from the Bible that show where God was wrathful—from the flood of Noah's time to the destruction of Sodom during Abraham's life. But I honestly can't reconcile the God of my experience with a God who acts cruelly. Further I cannot envision God rubbing His hands in sadistic joy as He sees a young man racked with pain in the last stages of the dreaded disease AIDS. To allow that would be to deny Christ's abrogation of the command "An eye for an eye, a tooth for a tooth." The God of my life is the God Isaiah describes as a loving mother unable to forget the child of her womb and the father of the prodigal son. That father is God patiently waiting for his prodigal son to return after the son had wished him dead and then squandered his inheritance.

In present-day society, many people have subtly developed a "hierarchy of sin" according to which sexual sins are the most abhorrent. We got a flavor of this in the downfall of Gary Hart. Although I in no way condone sexual immorality, I find that the stress on this sin allows sins of perhaps greater gravity to be considered as not all that important. As long as there is no sexual impropriety, many people think they can supply bullets to friends who kill people we don't like, stockpile nuclear bombs, ignore a dehumanizing farming problem, and shrug off racism as an issue of secondary importance. We must reach out to people with AIDS as Jesus reached out to lepers with the tenderness of love that is neither judgmental nor condescending. Like Him we must join our touch with prayers for healing. And added to our prayers should be support for the research that will bring a medical cure for AIDS.

Birth Control and Artificial Insemination

Why is the Catholic Church opposed to birth control?

In 1968 Pope Paul VI, in an encyclical or a teaching for the whole church called "Of Human Life," stated the church's position that "Each and every marriage act must remain open to the transmission of life." Bishops and theologians from around the world have striven to understand the fullness of the pope's words.

The pope's statement does not mean that the Catholic Church opposes birth control as such. A couple has the right and duty to control the number of births they generate. In a teaching from the Second Vatican Council, Catholic bishops stated that the decision to have children must take into account the welfare of the spouses and of their children; the material and spiritual conditions of the times; the couple's state in life; and the interests of the family group, of society, and of the church (*Pastoral Constitution on the Church in the Modern World*, n. 50).

A year before his encyclical "Of Human Life," Pope Paul VI stated in another encyclical called "The Progress of People" that "the population explosion adds to the difficulties of development . . . . Parents themselves must decide how many children to have. Parents themselves must consider their responsibilities before God and before each other, before their present children and before the community. Parents themselves must follow their consciences, formed by the law of God" (par. 37).

The church endorses a form of birth control called "natural family planning," which calls for intercourse only when the woman is biologically incapable of conceiving a child. That is clearly a form of birth control. Although many early attempts at determining the time of a woman's infertile period failed, in a somewhat haphazard method called "rhythm," thanks to extensive studies by the Billings and others, natural family planning is now said to be more effective as a method of birth control than the pill.

The Catholic Church opposes the intentional placing of a material obstacle to the conception of a child: e.g., a contraceptive pill, an intrauterine device, contraceptive foam, a condom. In the encyclical "Of Human Life," Pope Paul VI states what he thinks are the negative consequences of material obstacles to the conception of a child: conjugal infidelity, general lowering of morality, easy corruption of youth, loss of respect for women (n. 17).

When the encyclical "Of Human Life," was presented to the church in 1968, there were many voices of disagreement from priests, sisters, theologians, and the laity. Bishops from Canada and the Netherlands, while they supported the encyclical, spoke of a respect for a couple's decision to practice artificial contraception if they believed that action was God's will for them.

What is the Catholic Church's stand on sperm insemination, embryo and sperm banks, surrogate parenthood, and test-tube-baby technology?

The Catholic Church wants to foster love in marriages on physical, emotional, and spiritual levels. The act of sexual intercourse is a real symbol of all these levels of love between a husband and wife. Sexual intercourse is a sacred act of creation given to husband and wife by God. Since intercourse is the sacred way God has chosen to allow human life to come into the world, the church wants to insure that nothing interferes with this marriage act.

When modern science and medicine can generate life by isolating egg and/or sperm and then joining them apart from the sacred and natural act of intercourse, the official church asks that Catholics refrain from this way of generating life. The official Catholic Church opposes scientific or medical development that allows the creation of life in ways other than the joining of egg and sperm through the loving act of sexual intercourse.

Why does the Catholic Church oppose test tube fertilization for couples who can't have children by natural means?

I don't think the official church is being insensitive. Instead, it is calling us, in a loving way, to a greater good. The official church sees the seeming good of the generation of a human life by artificial reproduction as contrary to the mystery of God's gift of life.

I side with the Catholic Church as it beckons us to a drastic reevaluation of sexuality beyond the clinical, functional level. The life that comes from intercourse should not be something manipulated outside of sexual intercourse. The Catholic Church asks us to see intercourse as an act of love between husband and wife with God as an integral part of the life that is generated. The church wants us to let the verdict of life or no life be in the hands of the loving Creator.

Outside the context of faith and love of God, the official church's condemnation of artificial reproduction is difficult to understand.

One of the major causes of people's problems with the Catholic Church's teaching on artificial reproduction comes with a confusion in people's minds over the roles of science and religion. To comprehend the church's stand we must examine the relationship between science and religion.

As he probes with microscope and scalpel into the meaning of life, the scientist needs religion to remain aware of the mystery of God's presence in the world. There's a mystery in sexuality beyond the mere physical union of egg and sperm. The mystery is the ingredient of love—both God's and the married couple's. Religion needs science to place its mystical experience within practical limits. Biblical studies need the help of archaeologists and language scholars. Spiritual directors need the insights of psychologists to understand the human person. A large organized church needs the help of computer science. Religion and science must come together in their common striving for healing whether physical, emotional, or spiritual. As the church prays for a person dying of cancer, it also looks with hope and encouragement to scientists who are opening the door to a cure.

But a practical question arises. What's the difference between one scientist striving for a cure for cancer and another scientist striving to bring a child into the life of a couple who by themselves cannot have a child? One doctor wants to confront death. That's good. The other wants to create life. What can be wrong with that?

The official Catholic Church sees a difference between the healing of sickness and the generation of life. On the one hand, the church is supportive of today's scientists who are trying to overcome disease at all levels. This is in line with the actions of Jesus, who tirelessly strove to overcome illness through the healing of bodies, spirits, and souls.

Sexuality is another matter. Sex is an awesome, mysterious gift of God to us. To put the generation of life through the union of egg and sperm outside the context of sexual relations in marriage is going beyond our mortal privilege in dealing with God's gift of human life. It is this mystery of the gift of life that calls couples who cannot conceive to look to adoption and trust in God rather than artificial fertilization.

The official Catholic Church is taking a prophetic stance in its opposition to artificial fertilization. A true prophet is never accepted by the majority of people. The church is crying out against the profanation of life whether it's through war or the death penalty or abortion or pornography or creating human life through artificial means. The official Catholic Church is calling us to a sober reevaluation of marital love and sexuality. It is asking us to believe that if we do "what is natural" in sexuality, without artificial interference, we will have a proper relationship with Him who will bring to our lives peace, love, joy, and meaning.

What do you think of the controversy over frozen embryos?

I guess I'm getting old fashioned. I suppose I'm not as "with it" as I should be, but this story coming out of Maryville, Tennessee, has me shaking my head in disbelief.

Mary Sue and Junior Davis were married for nine years. One of their problems was that they couldn't conceive a child. To solve the dilemma, they went to a laboratory in Knoxville. There Junior masturbated in a temperature-controlled setting, and Mary Sue had eggs removed from her womb. A scientist joined the eggs and sperm, seven of them, and put them in cold storage till the couple was ready to implant them in Mary Sue. Several months later they decided to divorce. The plot thickened. Mary Sue wanted the right to implant the embryos in her womb and, I guess, have seven children. Junior didn't like that idea at all. He thought he should have the right to keep the embryos on ice.

Well, the judge, W. Dale Young, came down on the side of the woman. Not only does Mary Sue have the right to implant the embryos in her womb, the judge went even further. He said that human life begins at conception. And so embryos are not merely property, but human beings. The judge's thinking was really quite simple. What happened in the creation of these embryos was not the beginning of a monkey or a frog, but of a human being.

I suppose that I should be excited that there was a victory for the unborn. To be honest, I'm filled with deep sadness and fear. Something has gone wrong with our sense of values. The image of seven fertilized human eggs sitting in liquid nitrogen while mother and father are fighting for them in a court strikes me as obscene.

Did you see the futuristic Woody Allen movie *Sounder,* in which Woody is able to escape from the bad guys while holding a gun to the nose of the country's leader? The leader had been killed in an explosion several years before. His nose had been all that his followers had been able to salvage from the blast. They had kept the nose alive and were trying to clone it into the deceased leader. When Woody held the gun to the nose, his pursuers froze. I almost fell out of my seat with laughter. And then when Woody tripped in front of a steam-roller and dropped the nose, the result was a six-foot pancake. I howled.

The image of Woody Allen's nose came to mind as I read of the battle for the seven embryos. My laughter turned to sadness when I faced the fact that Junior and Mary Sue Davis are not fictional characters but real people. Something is going drastically wrong in our nation. I am sad and I am frightened. We are falling into dangerous aberrations in marriage and sexuality.

Now I do admit to a great deal of empathy for couples like Junior and Mary Sue who can't conceive a child. I can understand how they would want to conceive their own child rather than adopt one. But the alternative of masturbating and of removing eggs in a laboratory, of then joining them in a test tube and then storing them in liquid nitrogen, makes me shake my head in disbelief. Then these human embryos cool their heels while Mom and Dad decide if they want them to continue their development after they, the couple, are divorced.

Am I too romantic about sex? Perhaps. I see the conception of a child as a God-given gift that needs to be kept in the committed intimacy of intercourse in marriage.

We are going haywire. We are losing touch with God's part in giving children to married couples. Life, human life, should not be generated through a scientist's test tube.

Science and religion need to respect each other. I think that science as seen in test-tube conception has overstepped its bounds. In doing so, science is profaning our most sacred God-given gift of creation.

Why is pornography bad?

Pornography is a distortion of the beauty, mystery, and wonder that are a part of God's gift of creation. With the exploitation of sexuality we lose the sense of reverence and respect for our bodies. We must be careful that sexuality remains something special between two committed people. With the rapid increase of pornography in magazines and movies, on billboards and television, we lose the sense of sex being something special.

When pornography is allowed to become a "normal" representation of human sexuality, sex becomes nasty and dirty.

One of the greatest dangers of pornography is that it causes people to be regarded as things. Although the current cry is for sexual freedom, the reality is that those depicted in a pornographic way become slaves and objects to gawk at; they lose their sense of being special. Jesus opposed those who wanted to use others. He came to deal with people as special persons, not objects.

The opposite of pornography, puritanism, is not correct either. To be negative about one's body is not proper. The human body is magnificent; art that depicts the human body in a positive manner should be encouraged. It's twisted thinking that puts fig leaves on the works of masters.

Is masturbation permitted?

Masturbation is an act that is centered on oneself, an act of self-gratification. The proper place for sexual stimulation is with a marriage partner.

Some psychologists and professional people say that masturbation is a natural action. It is hard to deny that high percentages of people have masturbated.

When people come to me confessing to having masturbated one time or even having fallen into an almost addictive habit of frequent masturbation, I try to be as understanding and patient as possible. Condemnation and guilt from me frequently leaves a person with such a bad self-image that, I find, he is prone to commit the sin again. In most of the cases I have dealt with, masturbation is merely a symptom of personal frustration.

In our society in which magazines, television, films, and billboards are vying to get our attention through high levels of sexual attraction, masturbation is a way many people deal with the stimulation and the frustration of the media.

Masturbation happens often with people who feel the frustration of not having loving friends. A person who is frustrated at not being able to have sexual relations in marriage may masturbate. Masturbation frequently happens at times of tension.

I ask people to deal with the frustration that is causing the masturbation. Once a person can realize the danger of being manipulated by the media's sexual stimulation or develop meaningful friendships or find a marriage partner or face the reason for tensions, the masturbation problem fades.

Beyond the human level, we need to pray to God to get help in overcoming life's frustrations. He is the key to our peace and freedom.

Abortion

Where do you stand on abortion?

My heart aches when I see thousands of women and men marching in favor of abortion or when I read of a poll that says that over 70 percent of Americans favor abortion under certain circumstances. My first concern is the disregard for the living baby in the womb. The thought of burning with saline solution or slicing up and then sucking out that living human baby afflicts my sense of justice.

On yet another level, when I see women mobilizing to make sure they can maintain the legal right to have abortions, I fear we are losing touch with one of the greatest blessings a nation can have: the selfless love of a mother for her child.

I hear three main arguments from pro-abortion advocates: (1) "A woman should have the right and freedom to say whether she keeps or throws away the baby in her womb"; (2) "If *Roe v. Wade* is struck down, abortions will become life-threatening, back street, coat hanger, and butcher experiences"; and (3) "After a rape, an act of incest, or any irresponsible act of intercourse, a conceived child should be eliminated rather than be forced to live as an unwanted human being."

I too believe in freedom, and yes, individual freedom. A woman should have the freedom to choose her own husband, the school she would like to attend, a career, a car, a political candidate, and a religion. But that freedom doesn't spill over into the right to kill a baby in the womb. No amount of soft-pedaling the reality of a baby in the womb by referring to him or her as merely an embryo or an unwanted pregnancy or a tissue growth, can evade the fact that there is a growing human life in the womb. If properly cared for, the baby will grow into an adult human being like you and me. No person should be "free" to kill that baby.

I think that most people in our country oppose abortion. They don't like to see babies thrown in trash cans. Most Americans see this practice as detrimental to motherhood and against our sense of justice. Yet when people hear of a child conceived after rape or incest, their hearts harden, and they say such unwanted children should not be forced to come into the world. They speak of concern for the child and the mother.

What if the act of intercourse is not of love but of rape or simple sexual gratification? Or what if the couple would make a bad world for their child?

I find that people who put forth this argument in favor of abortion are sincere in their aversion to the injustice of rape and incest. I share their aversion. Nevertheless, I believe that rape and incest are not as detestable as the killing of a baby in the womb. Is death a better alternative?

The rapist has done an act of despicable injustice to the woman. Still, the responsibility to the generated life is more important than the way the life is generated.

The fertilized egg—even after rape—may not be eliminated. One act of injustice cannot be rectified by another act of injustice. Also, if the parents' prospects of giving the child a happy life are not good, we should work on improving those bad conditions rather than ending the life of the baby. True freedom comes only when we embrace responsibility, even when it is painful.

I believe that abortion is wrong. I pray that we will grow in our appreciation for freedom and life.

Does the fifteen-year-old girl who has just found out that her boyfriend "got her pregnant" have any freedom?

If freedom means doing whatever we like to do, then the girl has the freedom to run away from her fear of telling her parents. She doesn't have to give up the carefree joys of high school, sports, and all the normal facets of adolescence. She can turn away from the twenty-year commitment a mother must face in bringing a child into the world.

If freedom means doing what I feel like doing, I would be inclined to urge her to choose an abortion to guard her freedom. After all, who wants confrontation with parents and possible rejection? Who wants to lose those important years of growing up? And most of all, who wants to go through the pain of birth, of changing diapers, of sleepless nights, extra bills, and years of raising an intractable teenager? Then too there is so much talk of the homeless, of incest, and of wife battering. Who wants to bring a baby into a world like that?

But pro-abortion people are confusing freedom with license. License speaks of freedom without restraint. License dictates a freedom without responsibility to others. License puts a priority on what feels good for me. License is an extreme of freedom. No, an aberration of freedom.

The precious freedom of which I am so proud as an American must be continually guarded or a distorted idea of freedom or of selfish license will threaten it. The freedom I love is hedged around with commitments, restrictions, and responsibilities.

Do you think the soldiers who died through the years did so because it felt good? The price they paid with their blood for freedom can't be frittered away by self-seeking license.

Don't you hear me? I must have the freedom to choose what happens in my body!

To you women who are marching and working to maintain what you consider freedom, I admire your commitment and sense of responsibility. I know you are concerned about pregnant women not having to be restricted by an unwanted child. I know the pull to be free from possible poverty, injustice, and abuse. I hear your concern that an unwanted child is worse than a dead child. I too shudder at the thought of a back-alley abortion performed with a clothes-hanger. Such violence is abhorrent.

The solution is not abortion. We must be committed and responsible as a nation to changing the circumstances that seem to make abortion inevitable to those planning to undergo it. To agree with abortion "because it is always going to be with us" is a complete cop-out. If we follow that argument, we must permit stealing, cheating, and murder because they will always be with us.

To solve the abortion problem, we must strive to stop the conception of unwanted children. We must join forces in the more painful task of fostering a mature understanding of sex and commitment in marriage. We must strive to eliminate all kinds of physical and mental abuse. We ought to work at improving economic conditions for people birthing and raising children.

I don't agree with abortion. But in certain circumstances, like incest or rape, a woman must have her freedom!

The Catholic bishops of Great Britain were asked to respond to the problem of a woman who is a victim of rape or incest. They said that as long as she had not ovulated and her egg hadn't been fertilized by the unwelcome sperm, she could have the sperm removed from her womb by a doctor. Since abortion only involves a fertilized egg, this is not an abortion.

Doctors tell me that conception does not ordinarily occur immediately in the act of intercourse. The sperm may lie for two or three days in the mucus of the woman's vagina.

If the young girl delays the removal of the sperm to the time doctors say the egg has been fertilized by the sperm, then I would have to tell her that she can not abort the life in her womb.

An independent life is generated when the egg is fertilized while at the same time it is dependent on its mother. Despite the despicable circumstances of this life's beginning in rape, we shouldn't allow another despicable act to end that life.

But why should the mother, the victim of injustice, have to bear the burden of a child because of abuse by a man?

I recently met a young mother who learned that she had been conceived during an act of rape by her uncle. Despite this terrible beginning, the mother is a gift of love to her husband and three children. She is very active in serving the Lord and those in need. If her mother had been in favor of abortion after rape and incest, she would never have been able to be the wonderful person she is today.

Generally, I must tell you that I deeply resent your smug, insensitive, and chauvinistic attitude toward women and their struggle for justice, freedom, and self-respect.

I'm sorry I'm coming across to you this way. In response to your honest questions, I am trying to understand your need to have the freedom to choose abortion. I honestly don't think you are in favor of abortion. A woman is made to love and cherish the baby in her womb. Why do you want to reject your child so violently?

I feel there's something deeper going on here. As a woman you have suffered such injustice and humiliation at the hands of men that you are ready to wage a pitched battle against this latest onslaught on your freedom. Lawmakers, who are 99 percent men, will no longer treat you paternalistically. And so you say, "No!" to the Supreme Court. "No!" to the Congress. And "No!" to the Catholic Church, which is governed exclusively by men.

You've helped me to understand that I'm probably not going to convince you by my arguments against abortion and about sexual matters. I'm going to have to change my attitude toward you and then strive to get others, and especially the Catholic Church to give you the justice, freedom, and dignity you deserve before we can really talk.

Are you one of those "single-issue voters," who will vote for any candidate who is against abortion?

Some people consider being a "single issue voter" very important. Convinced that abortion is the ugly murder of innocent children, they can do nothing less than strive to protect the precious lives of children in the womb.

They are more concerned about a judge's and a politician's stand on abortion than about his belief in any other issue. Single issue voters feel that to ignore this frightening problem would be similar to ignoring the Jewish holocaust.

Although I am diametrically opposed to abortion and want to do all that I can to stop a mother's legal access to this evil, I find problems with blindly favoring or disregarding a politician or judge merely on the "single issue" of abortion.

If you join me in a desire to stop abortions, we need to admit that there are many legal factors to be dealt with, along with the need to end legal abortions in our country. For example, the economic factors that force a family or a single parent to undergo frightening financial difficulties in raising children are a vital contributor to the evil of abortion. The abuse of drugs and alcohol is a killing reality, which is adding to a milieu that disregards life. When there is a selfish addiction to drugs or drink, the life of the unborn child can easily become secondary. As we listen to the advertising which calls us to live beyond our needs, a child can seem to be a hindrance. And when a child is conceived in an unwanted atmosphere, where are the support systems in society to insure that the mother can have a safe pregnancy if she chooses that option? Finally, are we making it easy for couples who are unable to have their own children to adopt unwanted babies?

Other equally important abuses of human life are going on in our society and must be addressed. One Catholic cardinal calls these issues a "seamless garment" that can't be divided. If I am concerned with the life of the unborn, I can't ignore the lives of the elderly, those threatened by war through nuclear buildup or by the death penalty, and the crying needs of those dying of hunger. If a politician is pro-life but in favor of a disproportionate nuclear bomb buildup or euthanasia, I would pause before voting for him or her.

Let's don't be lazy voters who easily write off a politician because of one issue. Let's continue to stand firm against abortion but intelligently realize that abortion is often caused by many factors that need to be addressed on many fronts. Let's demand respect for all life.

Issues That Foster Life

Why are Catholic bishops so opposed to the death penalty? Doesn't the Bible say it is all right?

The death penalty is certainly permitted in the Bible. Such executions, though, were performed only when there was an urgent necessity and the good of society in general was at stake.

In our present society we have a relatively good sense of national security. An act of murder by a jealous husband or a deranged mass murderer does not mean the imminent collapse of our society. Today, in our society, I oppose the death penalty.

My opposition to the death penalty stems from my conviction of the sacredness of human life. This standard must be upheld despite the disregard for that life shown by the criminal.

I think that the demand for the death penalty on the part of so many betrays a vengeful sickness that is not worthy of our noble country. By answering killing with killing we allow the evil of killing to continue. We surrender ourselves to the ugly passion we so abhor in the murderer.

When faced with the law, "An eye for an eye and a tooth for a tooth," Jesus responded with a new law: "Do not take revenge on someone who does you wrong." That is inflammatory talk, especially in the face of the brutal murder of an innocent person, but Christ backed up his words when He forgave rather than cursed those who crucified Him.

When we speak of forgiveness as Christians, we often forget an important ingredient: *responsibility*. To forgive a person for an action is not to ignore the implications of that action. If you're a Catholic and you steal a hundred dollars and then ask for forgiveness, you can certainly be forgiven, but a condition of that forgiveness is the responsibility of returning the hundred dollars with interest.

A murderer must also pay a price. Someone who is deemed a continual threat to society must be incarcerated for the rest of his or her life if necessary.

In our penal system, unfortunately, most perpetrators of crime are punished by incarceration, but they are not obliged to bear the responsibility for their crimes. What is needed is an organization in prisons that will allow prisoners to work and get a paycheck to support the dependents of those they have killed. Regretfully, our prison labor force is a threat to other businesses, and so this plan of responsible restitution for crimes runs into a lot of opposition.

The Christ I experience in the Bible is not so naive as to say society doesn't need protection from murderers. I believe He wants us to make every effort to insure freedom, peace, and security for ourselves and those we love. Opposition to the death penalty does not mean that we become lax with criminals. I find the enthusiasm for the death penalty in some ways similar to the mentality that fosters abortion. Both acts betray a disrespect for life. We must stop this escalation of killing, or we will soon find ourselves in a vortex from which we cannot escape.

What's wrong with euthanasia? If a person is so sick or old that he or she can no longer be useful in life, shouldn't he or she be able to choose death?

My understanding of life is that it is an ongoing gift from God. We have no right to kill another or ourselves or allow someone to kill us.

Why should a person have to suffer? If medical aid can't take away the pain,

then a person should have the freedom to choose death.

What's so wrong with pain? Pain is a very important ingredient of life. Sometimes pain is the context in which we separate right from wrong. When a child runs into the street without looking, the pain of the parent's swat on the rear end is the child's source of learning to avoid an unnecessary danger.

Beyond physical pain there is emotional pain like that connected with leaving home or taking a new job. If we always fled this pain, we would stunt growth and development. There is also good in "religious pain." I mean by this the wrestling we do to understand God. For instance, we might doubt His existence or have a hard time reconciling the lives of His followers with the way we think life should be lived. This painful struggle is a valuable way of reaching the truth about God.

Pain can also have a powerful effect on another spiritual level. Catholics believe in a reality called "the Mystical Body of Christ." Through the power of the Holy Spirit, all baptized people are united to Christ and each other in a spiritual bond. We are united as parts of a body. Because of this union, a pain that I suffer here in California can be a source of healing and strength for an unseen Christian suffering in Africa. Pain and suffering can have a sacrificial effect, which brings healing and salvation to a person on the other side of the world.

In line with the idea of the Mystical Body is a thought St. Paul gave us in his letter to the Colossians. In chapter 1, verse 24, he says, "I fill up what is lacking in the sufferings of Christ." In a mysterious way Paul's suffering, after Christ's agony and death, was united to the Lord's pain. Paul's suffering became part of the "incomplete suffering" of Christ.

To me the verse says that Christ wants the suffering of Christians to be an integral part of His salvific suffering. What a dignity and power Christ gives to suffering.

To see a positive value in pain does not mean that we shun medicine or stop research to overcome disease. No, we must strive to overcome sickness. Jesus Himself was committed to freeing people from all kinds of illnesses. And he commissioned His followers to continue His healing. So in both prayer services and hospitals we strive to overcome sickness.

Although we don't embrace pain in a masochistic way, we do need to get a more positive perspective on its value. We must be on guard lest we lose the worth of pain in a hedonistic desire for pleasure. A healthy respect for pleasure *and* pain is a sign of good balance. Through pain we are purified and empowered to join our suffering with Christ's for the salvation of others.

There's a difference between pain we choose, like the pain of conditioning to play sports, and the pain of cancer. Still, both pains, in the Catholic view, can be efficacious for members of the Mystical Body of Christ. (That's easy to say when I am experiencing no pain! Nevertheless, I believe it.)

Morality in the U.S.A.

Is the United States a Christian country?

I love my country and feel that God has given us a special blessing of freedom and prosperity, but I am not blind to the abuses that have arisen amongst us. Segments of our own nation suffer injustice. In our foreign policy—our economic, military, and political dealings with other countries, we often fall short of Christ's command to love our neighbor as we love ourselves.

Christians should not be ashamed to bring Jesus' values into the actions of our nation. Since Jesus stands for values that can only make our country better, His selfless love, His courageous speaking of the truth, and His strong concern for the underprivileged can bless our country.

What do you think concerns Jesus about our nation?

I think He would be concerned with the high number of unemployed and homeless. He would want to get rid of poverty, not only from among the lower classes but now from among the middle classes when often both husband and wife, to the detriment of their children, have to work just to make ends meet.

I don't think Jesus would be opposed to a healthy defense budget. Just as there are criminals who must be constrained by police and jails, there are immature nations we must defend ourselves against lest we lose our liberty. I think, though, that Jesus would strike a better balance in allotting money for defense and for the poor.

In the struggle to maintain our high standard of living in the U.S., we must make sure that our level of comfort is not obtained at the price of injustice to people in third world countries. This desire to make use of cheap labor and to invest in third world countries can lead to financial and military support of oppressive governments.

Should an American Catholic endorse sending military equipment to a Central American country like El Salvador?

Christians should be in the forefront of making sure that we give the best our country has to offer to help people in El Salvador and other third world countries. We have been blessed with abundant crops. We should share that blessing. We have trained our citizens in occupations that can be a great service to underprivileged people. We should send educators, medical people, farmers, and missionaries to El Salvador.

Unfortunately our aid to these countries has an unhealthy stress on military weapons. I can't imagine Jesus saying to a government official in a third world country, "I can't help you first hand with your troubles, but here are some guns. Kill off the people who are oppressing you and causing problems. Everything will be fine."

If weapons from our country are killing people, we really are as responsible for the killing as if we had pulled the trigger ourselves. We should influence our government to care for the needs of other countries with Christ's love.

A few years ago, I spent some time in Nicaragua. I was with an ecumenical group of religious leaders. In a discussion with a leader in the government I found that approximately two thousand Cuban teachers had gone into the remote areas of Nicaragua to bring learning to a needing people. Only one thousand U.S. volunteers were doing similar work.

How embarrassing for us Americans! There were more people from a country whose government professes atheism than from our country that's proud to be God fearing.

Several Catholic leaders have come out in favor of "sanctuary" for illegal aliens. Please explain this.

Sanctuary can be found among the Egyptians, the Hebrews, the Greeks, the Romans, and the barbarian nations. The concept of sanctuary arose out of the need to prevent mob violence and family blood feuds. By fleeing to a shrine or temple sacred to a god, the accused or guilty party obtained immunity within the precincts of the sanctuary until the demands of justice could be met.

Today, various Catholic churches offer sanctuary to people who have fled their country for fear of their lives. When the government opposes the harboring of such illegal immigrants, the church offers the argument that Christians must protect those whose lives are in danger or whose religious freedom could be taken away.

Although certain legal precedents are offered by the church to justify going against government directions, the church's main argument is a moral one.

The church should not offer permanent sanctuary to persons who are fleeing a just punishment for crimes they have committed. And so when General Noriega fled to the Vatican Embassy, even though the Vatican had the legal right as a sovereign state to keep the General from prosecution, church leaders eventually persuaded him to leave and to be accountable for the crimes of which he was accused.

Politics and the Church

What is liberation theology?

One of the strong directives that came from the international meeting of bishops at the Second

Vatican Council in the early 1960s was that the church needed to follow Christ more closely in His love for the poor.

In 1967 the bishops of Central and Latin America met in Colombia to apply these teachings of the Vatican Council to their immediate needs. These Bishops faced the fact that the Catholic Church in their countries gave more attention to the rich and the powerful than to the poor. The bishops made a resolution to start giving a "preferential option for the poor" as Jesus had done in His public ministry. The decision seemed simple enough, but when the bishops started to put their resolve into action, they faced serious obstacles.

Several Latin American theologians developed a theology to help explain this option for the poor. They labeled it, "liberation theology."

The liberation theologians examined Scripture to find that Jesus wasn't concerned only with getting people to heaven.

I think Christ was balanced in His concern for heaven and earth. Certainly He called people to remember that everlasting life was important. Nevertheless, He was also concerned with curing sickness and with confronting lawyers and religious leaders who were putting unjust burdens on people. When He saw people hungry, He fed them. In Matthew 25, He said that the key to attaining heaven is feeding the hungry, clothing the naked, visiting the sick, and giving hospitality to strangers. He was concerned with justice, health, peace, and happiness for all while we are on this earth. Christ was a liberator! The church needs to balance a concern for preaching about heaven with making sure that people have at least basic needs for their everyday life: private property, work to support a family, education, medical care, housing, and food. When these basics are not supplied to the poor, liberation theology tries to show how supplying them is part of the following of Christ.

In Latin America the "option for the poor" meant that the church had to confront governments and big businesses, which exploited the poor. The ensuing insecurity of the governments and big businesses led them to acts of violence, and even killing, against church people. The list of murdered priests, Sisters, and active church lay leaders grew rapidly. Archbishop Oscar Romero of El Salvador was murdered in cold blood while he celebrated Mass.

In the face of violent injustice, some priests took up arms. This reaction was roundly condemned by the official church. Liberation theology is opposed to violent means. Its call is to imitate Christ's loving, nonviolent approach.

Although the world of Latin America may seem far away, we as U.S. citizens are deeply involved in it through business, economic aid, and arms dealing. We must have our Christian input into our government's involvement and make sure we are not party to the frustration of the liberation of our brothers and sisters in Latin America and in nations around the world.

Is Communism the greatest evil in the world?

Given the downfall of Communism in Eastern Europe and its faltering in Latin America, we can better see what a suppressive unjust form of government it is. We see the enormity of its evil as people flee from its subjection. How did it arise to such prominence? Why does it still have a stonghold in such places as China and Vietnam? We must never forget Communism's subtle attraction and make sure it is never allowed to seduce people again.

On the surface, Communism seems to offer many positive directions for how to live one's life. In a world where one small class of people unjustly dominates another, Communism speaks of doing away with oppressive classes. In a country where the majority of people are not well-fed or well-educated or able to receive proper medical help, Communism shouts out for a general sharing of food, education, and medical help.

As I look at countries where Communism has arisen, I find that frequently an elite suppressive government had previously withheld a fair sharing of food, housing, education, and medical care from the masses. For some, Communism seems the logical answer to their problems.

Despite the sharing of common goods, which Communism calls for, the system has serious drawbacks. In order to attain this common sharing, according to Communists, violent revolution is inevitable. All people are forced to give up their ownership of personal property. Along with shared material things, Communism demands a sameness in thinking. This is maintained by strict control of information. Artistic freedom is curtailed lest it breed diversity and thus lead to a lack of control by the authorities.

This need for control "for the common good" brings forth leaders who become insensitive to the needs of the individual and prefer the good of the masses.

Communism, as proposed by Marx, Lenin, and Mao, utterly suppresses religion. For Communists, belief in God encourages too much diversity and freedom of creation. Rather than allow the plurality of religious beliefs as we know them in the U.S.A., Communism opts for the uniformity of atheism.

The Catholic Church is strongly in favor of a concern for people who suffer injustice from a lack of food, unemployment, little access to education, and inadequate medical care. As Christians we need deep concern for the poor and oppressed.

But Catholicism parts company with Communism in their belief that violent revolution is the key to changing social injustice. The church stands up for the rights of all people to own land privately, to choose their line of work, and to be free to say what they believe even if this runs counter to government policies. When people can't worship God as they see fit, the church protests.

As the church speaks out against suppressive, atheistic Communism, it speaks words of praise of the freedom granted by the U.S. Constitution. But, as with any good thing, there is a danger of corruption. Capitalism can suppress people's rights if it looks only for financial gain and not the needs of the people it employs to make that gain.

How can our nation trust other countries, especially the Communists?

Recently Pope John Paul II urged world leaders to let mutual trust be the foundation of bringing an end to the nuclear arms race. In our insecurity we shudder at the implications of what the pope calls us to do as a nation. The pope is asking us to change a pattern of distrust that has become ingrained in our national thinking. You may respond, "Doesn't the pope know the intrinsic evil of

Communism and of those who follow its beliefs?" Interestingly enough he knows more about the terror of Communism than most Amercians. He has lived and worked under a Communist government for most of his life. But he sees the threat of nuclear incineration as the wrong response to Communism.

When the pope calls for greater trust, he is not ignorant of broken treaties and betrayed trust. He knows firsthand the danger of a dehumanizing philosophy like Communism. I feel confident that he is much more opposed to the evils of Communism than most of us in the United States.

So why is he calling us to his greater level of trust in our international relations? Quite simply, the alternative to no trust is an insane stockpiling of nuclear bombs that is bound to lead to an eventual catastrophe that will kill millions of people—including you and me.

On a spiritual level, I believe that trust is more powerful than a nuclear bomb. Trust builds enriching confidence, which allows people to listen to and even appreciate one another.

Christians are dogged by a demand to trust others. Jesus set the pattern by His tireless entrusting of others with His love. His love was a vulnerable giving of Himself into the hands of seemingly unworthy people. Although Christ was let down repeatedly, He kept trusting. Peter denied Him three times, yet Christ forgave him. The apostles fled from Jesus when He was taken prisoner, yet into these men's hands He entrusted the continuation of the kingdom He preached.

Trusting on an international level when national security is at risk is never easy. Our trust must not be a foolish surrender of freedom and rights. We must strike a balance between security and trust. This will open the door to a world that is not doomed to the threat of nuclear annihilation. It's salutary to remember the words of St. Augustine: "Never fight evil as though it arose entirely outside of yourself."

I believe that the pope's formula of greater trust is the key to an effective lessening of the tensions among the nuclear powers. I am speaking of a trust that is filled with a hope that the frightening overkill in the nuclear weapons buildup can be turned around.

Should a Christian run for political office?

A person who can bear the pressure of politics will have a high platform from which to proclaim the good news on both national and international levels. I encourage Catholic lay people to become active members of a political party as long as they remember they are subject to God's power. "Blessed are they who hunger and thirst for righteousness" (Matt. 5:6).

Politicians are able to pass legislation that will foster justice, peace, and unity. Politicians can help usher in the kingdom of God by speaking for and giving direction toward the truth. Good laws originate in God's justice, while bad laws hinder His justice.

Today many politicians struggle with the obligation to serve the needs of their people while at the same time be faithful to the call of their conscience and their church. Although politics can be a good tool for justice, it can be dangerous because one is dealing with money, power, and influence—all of which can corrupt. Getting the votes to stay in office, means that a politician needs to act in a way that pleases the majority of his constituency. A politician who feels the need to go against the majority because of the call of conscience should be courageous enough to do that and face the possibility of not being reelected. I am thinking particularly of a politician taking a stand that is pro-life in contrast to the majority of voters who may be pro-choice. I find no incongruity in a Catholic stating during a campaign that he or she is going to follow a proposed plan of action.

Is there something wrong with a politician's being pro-choice?

A woman's right to choose is a fundamental freedom that the Catholic Church wants to foster and protect. The problem comes when a woman chooses an action that restricts the right to freedom of another person. The Catholic Church believes that abortion kills an innocent child in the womb. A Catholic may not have an abortion.

The Catholic bishops in the United States have taken a strong stand against abortion. They believe that abortion is the killing of an unborn child. Many bishops believe that a Catholic politician who encourages, condones, or facilitates this murder is guilty of such a public scandal that the right to share Communion with other Catholics is in question.

Many bishops believe that the role of a Catholic politican is to move constantly in the direction of eliminating abortion.

Despite that belief, the church cannot restrict a person who is not a Catholic from choosing to have an abortion.

In this case, the church and Catholic politicians can only offer what they believe in opposition to abortions with the hope that those committing abortions will understand that what they are doing is evil.

What about Catholic politicians getting involved in the inevitable political compromises?

Of course compromises will have to be made in politics. We don't live in a world where the good of God's kingdom can always come to pass overnight. I believe that as long as a politician is acting in accord with his or her Christian convictions, compromise is permitted. For example a Catholic politician working for the life of the unborn could agree to legislation that would merely limit abortions. Such a stand would be better than one that allowed abortion on demand.

What about the separation of church and state?

I am very much in favor of the separation of church and state. I shudder at the thought of a situation like that in Iran happening in the U.S. In Iran some religious leaders are government officials. Religious leaders should not hold political office. In our country, the pluralism of religious beliefs needs to be respected.

I can understand the need to restrict an exclusively Christian Christmas scene from in front of a federal building. As Catholics, we must be sensitive to the beliefs of Jews and Muslims who can easily be offended.

The church's stand for pro-life legislation has an unfair influence on those who are not Catholic.

Abortion is a human moral issue before it can be

217

connected with the tenets of a religious denomination. I don't think a "pro-life" stance is primarily
religious. It is morality on a simple human level.

**You say that you want to keep the
separation of church and state. I don't
believe it. A quick look at history shows
that Catholic politicians, kings, priests,
bishops, and popes have wielded great
political power to foster Catholic
interests. Do you want to get back into
power?**

Yes, you are certainly correct in your reading of
history. The Catholic Church hierarchy and even
the laity have wielded great political power at
times.

I can only respond by saying that the Church
has realized the folly of its ways and is now moving
to a sensitivity to others' freedom to worship and
believe as they will. Since the Second Vatican
Council, there has been a definite endorsement by
the church of the separation of church and state.
That of course doesn't mean that Catholics are not
working hard to foster religious freedom of expression and basic human rights.

To help maintain this separation of church and
state, the Vatican has promulgated a law that affects all clerics and even lay members of religious
communities. They may not hold any public office.
A religious leader is called upon to be a prophet, a
person who speaks God's words with great freedom. Although politicians certainly have freedom,
much of their day is spent in working out compromises to get the best legislation possible. A religious leader needs to be as free as possible from
all compromise.

That doesn't mean that the laity shouldn't be involved in politics. But just as Saul was challenged by Samuel and David by Nathan, so priests and bishops must be unencumbered by political expectations so that they can challenge politicans.

Why is the Vatican a sovereign state? You want the best of two worlds, religious and secular.

The Vatican is both the headquarters for the Catholic religion and a secular state. In the past the Vatican was a powerful secular force. The pope was head of the Papal States, which comprised a large part of present-day Italy. To maintain those states, the Vatican even had an army.

Although I can shake my head in disbelief that the church of Jesus could slip into taking on such material and militaristic power, an open look at history shows how this seeming incongruity developed.

One of the reasons for the Vatican's acquisition of land and power was the request for protection from the people of Italy. With the fall of the Roman Empire, there was no government or army to protect people from foreigners invading the country. People looked to the pope for protection.

Such healthy activity on the part of the church soon degenerated into political control and manipulation. In modern times, secular politicians and military personnel have taken their proper roles in Italy.

The only vestige of the Vatican States that is left is the present-day Vatican City. Its army is now the largely ceremonial Swiss Guard.

Should the Church give up its status as a temporal state? I think not. The secular state status allows the church to speak of Christian values beyond the religious sphere. The pope's meeting with leaders of different countries can foster cooperation and justice. The meeting of Gorbachev with the pope was facilitated by the Vatican's secular status.

With the Catholic Church's strong commitment to the separation of church and state, the Vatican State is not striving for temporal power. The Church is trying to bring the message of Christ's love and forgiveness into the lives of as many people as possible.

SECTION 5

Catholics and People of Other Beliefs

An examination of the Gospels shows that Jesus spoke more about the kingdom of God than about the church. Jesus' main goal was to proclaim the kingdom of God.

What is this kingdom? Simply put, the kingdom is the reign of God. The kingdom happens whenever and wherever the will of God is fulfilled. The goal of the Church is to proclaim the kingdom of God.

Jesus described the kingdom through many stories; the Kingdom of God is like a mustard seed or a wedding banquet. Those who are members of the kingdom follow the moral directives that Jesus gives; for example, they seek justice, love their enemies, and don't let laws get in the way of the people they should serve.

St. Paul describes the presence of the kingdom as "not a matter of food and drink, but of righteousness, peace, and joy in the Holy Spirit (Rom. 14:17).

In this chapter we will see Christ's goal for us to be members of the kingdom, but we will face the fact that our division as Christians and even our divisions as people who are trying to love the Father, be we Christian, Jew, or Muslim, seems to fall short of the unity of the kingdom.

The kingdom that Jesus preached is somewhat

elusive. Theologians speak of it as "here, but not yet." We can experience the "here" of the kingdom at times in our churches when there is peace, love, joy, and unity. Ah, but there are other times when we know we are far from the kingdom because of our turmoil, hatred, dread, and division. We need to work toward the reality of the kingdom as Christians and people of various religions.

Salvation

What do you believe about salvation?

Salvation is a gift I cannot do anything to earn. I believe Jesus has given salvation to me, but because of His gift of freedom, I can choose it or reject it.

Catholics believe in an objective as well as a subjective redemption. Objectively, the blood of Jesus has been poured out for me, and I have been saved. But subjectively, I am still able to turn away from the beautiful gift of salvation. In Hebrews 6:4 the writer spoke of people who joined the Christian community, were filled with the Holy Spirit, and then turned away from God.

Are you sure you are saved?

Certainly I know I am saved through the love relationship I have with Jesus. Nevertheless, I must work out my salvation in "fear and trembling," as St. Paul urges the Philippians in 2:12. When you ask a newly married couple if their love is strong and forever, they will say "Yes!" Divorce is unthinkable to them. My love for Jesus gives me an assurance not unlike the love of the newlywed. I know that Jesus loves me, that I love Him, and that we will live forever.

Nevertheless, I know His great gift is held by me

in a fragile vessel. I know I am free and inclined toward evil. I have no question about God's faithfulness toward giving salvation. My response to that gift is what is tenuous and in need of tender fostering. Like the "secure" love of the newlyweds, without constant nurturing, it can be lost.

I am not filled with dread of what might happen to me. I have an overriding peace that God loves me as the father loved the prodigal son. His love is everlasting.

What is purgatory?

The Catholic Church defined the existence of purgatory at the Council of Florence in 1439 and also the Council of Trent. However, Catholics believed in the reality of purgatory long before these councils convened. The practice of praying for the dead can be found in liturgies from the early Christian era.

The council taught in accordance with Scripture (Num. 20:12; 2 Macc. 12:44) that God does not always remove all of the punishment for sin, even though the sin is forgiven. Nothing defiled can enter heaven (Wisd. Sol. 7:25; Isa. 25:8; Heb. 1:13; Rev. 21:7). Yet Christians often die with sins upon their souls. In their freedom they have failed to respond fully to Jesus. All those who die in sin or with punishment unpaid therefore must atone in purgatory.

We believe in Jesus' power to wash away our sins. We know we are completely forgiven through His blood. But to be forgiven and justified doesn't mean we can ignore our responsibility for what our sins have inflicted on others. The evil of our sin lives on in others while we are alive and after our death. This responsibility is fulfilled by us in purgatory and through the prayers and acts of reparation of those still on earth. This is why we pray for the dead at Mass.

Purgatory is not inevitable for everyone. Peter tells us that our responsibility for evil done can be overcome by prayer and action while we are still living on the earth, for "love covers a multitude of sins" (1 Pet. 4:8).

What is an indulgence?

Today indulgences do not have a prominent place in the spirituality of most Catholics. As Catholics strive to be more united with protestants, the church's abuse of indulgences at the time of the Reformation is an embarrassment to most Catholics. Unfortunately, the wholesome applying of Christ's merits to ourselves and others was tarnished in the past by the selling of indulgences.

In 1967 Pope Pius VI made a statement about indulgences that helped to clarify the part they should play in a Catholic's spirituality. The pope linked the doctrine of indulgences with the doctrine of the Communion of Saints, that the church on earth is united with the church in heaven and in purgatory. The church has access to the infinite and inexhaustible value which the merits of Christ have in the sight of God. An indulgence, he declares, is "the remission in the sight of God of the temporal punishment due to sins which have already been blotted out as far as guilt is concerned."

A Catholic can say prayers, do acts of penance, care for the needs of others, and thereby gain the remission of punishment for personal sins and the sins of others living and dead.

Do Catholics believe that they're the only ones who will go to heaven?

Catholics are asked to believe that their expression of Christianity is the truest expression of the church that began on pentecost Sunday and continues to the present day. The Second Vatican Council clarified the issue by saying, "The true Church subsists in the Catholic Church." The word *subsists* is significant because the bishops chose it to replace the word *is*.

If a person believes this in his conscience, but then rejects the church, he or she puts salvation into jeopardy. But if a person in his heart, does not see the Catholic Church as the true church, then he must follow his own conscience and worship God to the best of his ability. Under such a response to his conscience, he can attain salvation. That means a protestant, a Jew, or a Muslim can attain salvation by loving God as best he or she can.

Christ speaks of this form of salvation in the twenty-fifth chapter of Matthew. People who do not know they are meeting Christ do so when they visit a sick person, clothe the naked, give food to the hungry, and care for those who are in prison. These people who are invited into salvation protest that they didn't know Christ, the key to salvation. The Lord responds that a person who cares for the needs of another cares for Jesus.

Christian Unity

What is the meaning of the word *Catholic*?

The word *Catholic*, which I use to describe the community in which I make my commitment to

Christ, means universal. Catholicism offers a wide spectrum of possible forms of worship and life-style. In worship there are several rites other than Roman Catholic. There are Greek Catholics, Maronite Catholics, Melkite Catholics, Syrian Catholics, and others. Each of these rites has an ancient form of worship quite different than the Roman Rite in which I have been raised.

Even within the Roman Rite I find a great diversity of expressions of worship. A black Gospel Mass is filled with actions and music very different from a Vietnamese Eucharistic celebration. All of these differ from a quiet Sunday morning Mass that might be more meditative than social. Then, too, a Catholic can attend Sunday worship in Latin, the way Mass was said before the Second Vatican Council.

If I want to be a Catholic who lives as a hermit on a hill, that is possible. On the other hand, I can marry and have twelve kids. For a Catholic, unity is not total uniformity.

I feel prejudice against people of other denominations and other religions.

Prejudice often comes from personal insecurity. People of other beliefs are threats to a closed way of believing. Prejudice is overcome through the risk of dialogue and listening. We must work together on projects of common concern. When this happens, we appreciate other persons and their belief. This leads to unity.

Religious prejudice is often based on generalizations about people and doctrine. I urge you to interact with people of other denominations and faiths. Get beyond the past relationships among our faiths, which are often tainted with injustice.

Take the time to grow in love of a person of a different faith. We must be honest about the past. We must be vulnerable enough to share some of the aspects of our churches that need improvement. We might even go so far as to admit that we have made mistakes. Perish the thought! We might even say, "I'm sorry."

Why are Catholics and protestants so cold to each other?

Recently I've had the pleasure of spending several days in prayer and dialogue with members of different denominations. First I spoke at a convention of Lutheran, Anglican, and Roman Catholics called LARC in Sacramento, California. Then I made my annual retreat with a group of twenty other ministers who were from various denominations. Here in Southern California I have regularly participated on a panel with a protestant minister and a rabbi in a program called *Religion on the Line* on the popular ABC radio station.

The flood of ecumenical contact leaves me exhilarated and filled with the conviction that denominations and religions must continue to talk and interact. In the sixties and seventies dialogue about theological and social issues existed among Catholics and Greek Orthodox, Lutherans, and Anglicans. Lutherans and Methodists attained greater unity in their own denominations with mergers. In the last ten years or so, dialogue between different denominations has continued but not with the same intensity. I hope that ecumenical efforts move more into the spotlight.

One of the biggest problems with risking dialogue with people of different beliefs is that in our insecurity, we fear that our firm religious beliefs will be shaken. Yet in a wonderful way, when we dialogue, we grow not only in understanding of what we believe but also in unity with others. That is so important. To close off dialogue with others is to imply that they are not loved by God.

One of the most important aspects of dialogue is listening. Listening must be more important than trying to convince the other person to join a different denomination or faith. We can't deny that if we love our denomination or religion we desire others to share in our good fortune. Still, in my experience, overt evangelizaton with people who have already chosen a community of faith almost always leads to alienation. The goal of dialogue must be unity and not uniformity.

Most of the people who come knocking at my door to tell me about their religion lack listening skills. They don't see the good in the way I love God. They insist that I can only come to Him by joining their church. Evangelization should not be concerned with getting a person to change his religion. The goal is to offer your expression of faith freely so that another may choose or reject it.

I believe that we must respect a person's faith in God to the extent that we are relaxed that he will attain salvation in his own denomination or religion. As long as he responds to God to the best of his ability, he can be saved. As a Catholic I believe that salvation comes through Jesus. But Jesus can express Himself to others in ways that are richer and deeper than I can imagine or judge.

I urge you to do what you can to keep the flame of religious unity alive. Find the goodness in people of different faiths. We will know and love God better the more we can respect His presence in others.

How do you justify the Inquisition?

The inquisition is not something Catholics are proud of today. It arose out of a distorted desire to bring salvation to people who were not Catholic. One of the Scriptures that was used to justify the forcing of others to accept Christ was the story Jesus told of a banquet. When people declined to come to the banquet, the head of the household told His servants to go out and force people to come in (Matt. 22). Using this Scripture to coerce people to go against their conscience was a wrong interpretation of Scripture.

The Catholic Church has recently clarified the belief that all people are free to respond to the Lord in the way their consciences call them. Conversion is not a matter of force. At the command of Christ, Christians are called to spread the good news of Jesus to all people. This "spreading" is an offer that a person has a right to choose or reject.

Why don't Catholics permit non-Catholics to receive Communion at Mass?

For a Catholic receiving communion is a sign of one's commitment to the community of disciples of Jesus, with whom one is sharing the meal. A Catholic who receives communion says, "yes" to the authority of the leaders of the church, the sacraments and Catholic liturgy. A Catholic believes that Christ is present in the bread and wine. The Catholic communicant should be willing to commit to a specific Catholic community of worship.

If a non-Catholic is willing to make that degree of commitment, he or she may receive Communion. But as you see, that means that the person is really a Catholic.

On one level, allowing intercommunion would

encourage the union of churches. Most of us want that. Still, we should not easily gloss over the fact that there has been a separation in Christian communities. The pain of Christians not being able to share communion is great. This pain can be a healing incentive to strive for unity on those points that separate us.

The recent dialogue of Roman Catholic theologians with Anglican and Lutheran theologians has shown there is great uniformity of belief about the Eucharist. This bodes well for the future possibility of intercommunion.

Catholics and Non-Christian Religions

What do you think about the New Age Movement?

The New Age Movement universally proclaims that we are God and we created God in His own image. True to their belief that all is one, they consider men and women to be a part of the Godhead (the "cosmic consciousness" or the "force"). All a person needs to do is to discover and develop his or her divinity by expanding consciousness through meditation and other methods. Ultimately, we are on our way to godhood. It is even said that one may enter fully into the spirit of the God of Force. New Age people believe that God is a neutral force, which can be manipulated either for good or evil.

In contrast to the Bible, which says that "Just as it is appointed that human beings die once, and after this the judgment" (Heb. 9:27), death in its finality is denied. Instead the movement teaches reincarnation, a concept stemming from Hinduism and Buddhism. According to this teaching, a human being does not really die but is endlessly reborn into new life cycles. The form of reincarnation depends on how one spent one's previous life. This automatic "law of karma" remains in effect until a person perfects himself sufficiently to enter "nirvana," a state in which the individual ceases to exist.

The New Age Movement states clearly that a human being can save himself by finding his "higher self" through consciousness expansion. In other words, faith in human beings and in the all-pervasive energy or life force throughout the cosmos is at the center of the New Age spirituality. When a person desires to "be like God" (Gen. 3:5), I get nervous, for he is obviously opening the door to Lucifer.

The New Age Movement encourages forms of occultism such as communicating with the dead, conjuring spirits, clairvoyance, telepathy, and levitating objects by the power of thought.

Despite an initial attraction to the positive vision of how people can use their God-given gifts more effectively, I think a Christian should stay clear of this movement.

Why have Christians treated Jews so badly?

Antisemitism found its roots in words and attitudes conveyed in the New Testament, especially in the Gospel of John. John frequently seemed to use the word "Jews" in a pejorative sense. "Jews" were the people that opposed Jesus and instigated the process of His murder through the Romans. One of the strongest statements against Jews in the book of John records Jesus' saying, "You [Jews] belong to your father the devil and you willingly carry out your father's desires. He was a murderer from the beginning and does not stand in truth, because there is no truth in him. When he tells a lie, he speaks in character, because he is a liar and the father of lies" (John 8:44).

The Gospel of John was composed at a time when Christians were being ostracized by strict Jews. The anti-Jewish tone of this book reflects the antagonism Christians felt toward the Jews who were persecuting them.

The earlier three Gospels don't single out the Jews for scorn as John's Gospel does. St. Paul has the kindest words for the Jews: "In respect to the gospel, they are enemies on your account; but in respect to election, they are beloved because of the patriarch. For the gifts and the call of God are irrevocable" (Rom. 11:28—29).

During the fourth century, prominent Christian writers and preachers were merciless in their scorn of the Jews. St. Jerome upbraids Jews in his writings as serpents, haters of all men, and Judases. Their psalms and prayers, he states, are the "braying of donkeys," and they curse Christians in their synagogues.

St. John Chrysostom of Antioch spoke "of their rapine, their cupidity, their deception of the poor, of thieveries, and huckstering. Indeed a whole day would not suffice to tell all." He asks how Christians can dare "have the slightest converse" with Jews, "Most miserable of all men," men who are "lustful, rapacious, greedy, perfidious bandits." Are they not "inveterate murderers, destroyers, men possessed by the devil" whom "debauchery and drunkenness have given them the manners of the pig and the lusty goat? They know only one thing, to satisfy their gullets, get drunk to kill and maim one another." Indeed, "they have surpassed the ferocity of wild beasts, for they murder their off spring and immolate them to the devil." And why are Jews degenerate? Because of their "odious assassination of Christ."

St. Augustine, a contemporary of Chrysostom, is a bit more restrained. He agrees with Paul's special affection for the Jews as God's people. Still he writes that Judaism, since the death of Christ, is a corruption; indeed Judas is the image of the Jewish people, their understanding of the Scriptures is carnal, they bear guilt for the death of the Savior, for through their fathers they have killed Christ. In one of his sermons, Augustine explains, "The Jews held him, the Jews insulted him, the Jews bound him, they crowned him with thorns, dishonored him by spitting upon him, they scourged him, they heaped abuses upon him, they hung him upon a tree, they pierced him with a lance."

As one looks through history, one hopes for words of love and kindness coming from Catholic leaders, but they are few. In the sixth century Pope Gregory the Great, who was a spiritual and temporal ruler at a time of great chaos in Europe, demanded that Jewish legal rights be respected. Although he wanted Jews to become Christians, he opposed any kind of coercion in calling them to the church.

In 1965 Catholic bishops at the Second Vatican Council took a strong stand to turn around centuries of persecution and lack of Catholic respect for Jews. In a document called *Nostra Aetate* they stressed the common patrimony binding the church and Israel, deplored hatred and persecution of the Jew, forbade representing the Jewish people of ancient or modern times as guilty of the death of Christ, and called for fraternal dialogue and biblical studies between Christians and Jews.

Despite this giant step in opening the door for understanding and peace, there are still issues of contention. The Vatican does not recognize the state of Israel. The Vatican does not oppose a Jewish homeland, but will not endorse a nation whose borders are disputed as is the case with Israel. The Vatican doesn't recognize the state of Jordan for the same reason. The Catholic Church is very much concerned with the injustice suffered by displaced Palestinians.

When a group of Carmelite nuns made a convent out of a building within the walls of the former concentration camp at Auschwitz, the Jewish community objected. For Jews Auschwitz represents a time when God was silent to their needs. The presence of the praying nuns in the camp goes against the silence the Jews think should happen in the camp. With reluctance, the Catholic Church has agreed to relocate the nuns, but only after flashes of antisemitism from some church leaders.

Catholics hold a frightening record of treating Jews with scorn, humiliation, and injustice. I am full of hope for the future. There is a more healthy dialogue between Jews and Catholics now. I hope that we Catholics can grow in showing our Jewish brothers and sisters the love and respect they deserve in line with the deep love and honor they have from the Lord.

Why is it that people who believe in God—Christians, Jews, Hindus, and Muslims—seem to have problems getting along?

Most people who believe in God tend to develop unattractive blinders. "Because God loves me," they say, "I then conclude that He loves me more than a person of another religion or denomination. I can even conclude that He is displeased with people who don't relate to Him in the way I do."

This narrow, smug belief that God is on my side causes division and violence. If I believe that God is only with me, then I can kill, torture, segregate, and even start a war with those I believe are not in His favor. I can justify my actions by saying, "God is on my side." I believe that such religious prejudice is alive today here in the U.S.A. and not only in Lebanon and Iran.

The past we share with other denominations and religions is filled with prejudice, bloodshed, revenge, and hate. But I can't think of any better time than now to start opening the doors of dialogue with all non-Christians. We don't have much more to lose, but we have so much to gain.

One of the most devastating results of this God-is-on-my-side mentality is that as a Christian I can doubt the possibility of non-Christians' salvation.

I am happy to say that the Catholic Church has officially said in the documents of the Second Vatican Council, "Those who, through no fault of their own, do not know the Gospel of Christ or His Church but nevertheless seek God with a sincere heart and, moved by grace, try in their actions to do His will as they know it . . . achieve eternal salvation."

Are you contradicting Jesus' words that salvation comes only through Him?

This doesn't contradict Jesus' words in the Gospels that only through Him can one attain salvation. To one who believes that Jesus is God, Christ is the One through whom all God-seekers attain salvation. People encounter Christ in more ways than by hearing Him preached by a flesh-and-blood missionary. I believe that Jesus can come to people with the challenge of His truth and love in ways that are beyond missionary efforts. Jesus loves all of creation. He asks us to spread that love around the world. Until that can happen in fact, He brings His love and salvation to His creatures in His own special way.

To think otherwise, a Christian would have to say that a billion people who live in China today and will never hear of Jesus are doomed to hell. Millions of other people around the world know of Jesus but don't choose Him because of the un-Christian actions and thinking of His followers. To say such people are condemned contradicts my understanding of a just and loving God.

To say all that means an end to the missionary mandate that was so clear in Jesus' teaching.

This possibility of salvation for non-Christians doesn't mean that I abandon missionary work. Because I have been touched by the love of God in Jesus, I want to offer the fullness of that love to those I care for. My efforts need to take a different tack from the ones followed in the past. My attitude should be one of deep respect. I must study and get to know people who are not Christian. I must be open to learning from them other ways of coming closer to the Lord. I must seek to find God as He is among them.

I recently heard a rabbi ask Christians to try not

to convert Jews for the next one hundred years. I think there's deep wisdom in that sentiment. Although it is hard for a Christian to stifle enthusiasm for sharing Jesus, perhaps more efforts to appreciate where non-Christians are coming from will give more honor to God and help us realize that we are all His sons and daughters.

What are Catholics doing as foreign missionaries?

Missionary work has always been one of the main thrusts of the Catholic Church. Church history shows outstanding examples of men and women who have brought Christ to nations from Europe to Africa, from the Americas to Asia. The church is proud of such evangelists as Boniface in Germany, Francis Xavier in Asia, and Junipero Serra in California.

The work is continued today by thousands of missionaries from around the world working to evangelize all people.

Unfortunately the number of missionaries from the United States is quite low. Of the fifty-four million Catholics in the States, only some six thousand are working as overseas missionaries.

There are several reasons for this. In many nations Americans are considered "ugly" because of alleged government complicity in creating unjust conditions in third world countries, partly because of capitalistic manipulations. This negative image has hindered many would-be missionaries from enlisting.

I am sure that the Second Vatican Council's statement on religious freedom is also a factor in people's not choosing to undergo the rigors of missionary life.

Today Catholic Church leaders are deeply concerned about protestant missionaries who are going to people of Catholic background and turning them away from the church. We feel much of the same indignation that many Jews feel when Christians try to get them to convert to Christianity.

For many contemporary Catholic missionaries, the goal of evangelization is not to get people to change religions but to foster greater love and respect among people of different faiths. People should be encouraged to remain where they are and be the best Presbyterians, Assembly of God members, or Jews they can be. If, in the dialogue, a person decides to change from Catholicism to Judaism or from the Four-Square Church to the Methodist Church, we must respect a person's religious freedom.

What about Catholic missionary work here in the United States? For instance, there seem to be very few Catholics in the black community.

There are only 1.5 million black Catholics in our nation's total population of thirty million blacks. There are only about 320 black priests in the country.

When slavery was the accepted way of life for the majority of the people in our nation, prior to the Emancipation Proclamation, Catholic missionary work among the slaves was almost unknown. Although Catholic missionaries made great strides among native Americans across the country, the greatest influence among the slaves was the Methodist missionaries. That sowing of the seed so long ago is the reason we think of blacks being more protestant than Catholic.

When the institution of slavery was being debated most intensely, just before the Civil War, U.S. Catholic bishops still didn't think that taking a stand for blacks was important. They were very quiet when they had the chance to oppose slavery. Historians say that because Catholics were such a persecuted minority in the U.S. in the mid-1800s, the bishops feared political and physical reprisals if they spoke out. It wasn't until the great influx of immigrants in the late 1800s from Ireland, France, Germany, and Italy that Catholics felt more secure about voicing unpopular opinions.

But this didn't mean an increase of efforts to evangelize blacks. Into the 1900s most black men were, for all practical purposes, not encouraged nor permitted to enter seminaries to study for the Catholic priesthood. Not until 1920 did two German Divine Word missionaries open a seminary for blacks in Bay St. Louis, Mississippi.

The importance of evangelization still seemed to move at a snail's pace. Bishop Harold Perry of New Orleans, the first black Bishop in the States, was not ordained a bishop until the mid-1960s.

Although the number of black bishops has reached thirteen and the number of black Catholics has doubled in the last few decades, there is a need for drastic steps by the church to speak to the black (now African-American) community. The church has been, if not racist, then derelict in its efforts to call blacks to the Catholic Church. I am pleased that there is a current awakening in the Church to the fact that it needs to do more to minister to blacks.

So now you are going to get out there and start snatching up those black protestants to get them into the Catholic Church?

No, we have got to be true to the ideal of respect for others' beliefs and for their freedom of conscience that now is the foundation of evangelizing. The first aim for Catholics is to offer love and service to black Catholics. Then our attention will go to blacks who have no church affiliation.

What about missionary work among the new immigrants; among the Hispanics?

There is a projection that by the turn of the century, 50 percent of all Catholics in the States will be of Hispanic descent. The number of Catholics in the U.S. from countries like Mexico and Puerto Rico has increased dramatically in the last few years.

Unfortunately, the Catholic Church is not doing enough to care for their needs. Another statistic from the Catholic bishops says that sixty thousand Hispanics are leaving the Catholic Church and joining protestant denominations each year. To deal with this problem, the Catholic bishops are putting into action many concrete plans to minister better to Hispanic Catholics.

Their first priority is to encourage more young people to move into roles of leadership in the church. One of those roles is the priesthood. Because most seminaries in recent history were dominated by students and administrators who came from an Anglo-Saxon heritage, Hispanics were not inclined to join the seminary. They didn't feel that their culture was given the attention it deserved in the seminaries. Bishops are working to make seminaries more attractive to Hispanics.

In my own community, the Divine Word Missionaries, we dealt with the problem by starting a seminary in the middle of the Hispanic barrio of East Los Angeles. Casa Guadalupe is a college-training center for Hispanic men who can worship in Spanish and foster their cultural heritage. The seminarians must spend a minimum of twenty hours a week serving their Hispanic neighbors.

Across the country, priests are being urged to learn Spanish and offer the services of the church to Hispanics. Because of the low number of vocations to the priesthood, Hispanic laity are being asked to share the work of evangelization.

What about Orientals?

In the mid-seventies the U.S. had a sudden influx of large numbers of Vietnamese. Many of them are Catholic. Fortunately, they brought many priests with them. As a matter of fact, seminaries across the country boast large numbers of Vietnamese students. In a college seminary in Iowa, over 50 percent of the seminarians are Vietnamese.

The Vietnamese joined large numbers of Filipino, Indonesian, and South Korean Catholics in the U.S.

The Catholic Church in America is challenged to serve the needs of large numbers of Hispanic and Oriental Catholics who are streaming to our country every day.

The face of the Catholic Church in the United States is changing rapidly. Unfortunately the number of priests coming from the "European" background is dwindling. Today there are some thirty thousand priests ministering to the fifty-four million U.S. Catholics. Within ten years the number of priests will be cut in half. This is due to attrition—by death and by the departure of those who resign from the active ministry. The number of seminarians is about one-fourth of what it was in the mid-1960s.

Part of the solution to the problem is for priests to share with the laity the role of evangelizing. With fewer priests, many of the functions that formerly were performed by priests will now have to be performed by married deacons and members of the laity: baptisms, marriages, bringing Communion to the sick, conducting Sunday services, and even administering parishes.

Catholics will have to turn to the foreign mission countries and ask them to send us priests. Seminaries are full in such places as Indonesia, the Philippines, India, and South Korea. Interestingly, another place where priestly vocations are abundant is Poland.

The Catholic Church in the United States grew partly because of the influx of priests from Ireland, Germany, Italy, and France. Indications are that in the twentieth century, the church will grow primarily through a greater involvement of the laity in church life and because of the help of priests from the third world.

Catholics have so much money! Why aren't they on television like the protestant fundamentalists?

This seems to be a false statement since there is a general conviction that the Catholic Church is very wealthy. Lack of money is one of the main reasons Catholic evangelists are not on television.

Many times I have heard the statement, "If the Catholic Church wants to get onto TV, all it has to do is tap some of its unlimited funds and move into the ranks of the presently successful protestant evangelists."

The wealth of the Catholic Church is very deceptive. Of course there are many fixed assets: church buildings, schools, and hospitals. The problem is that running these institutions often costs more money than Catholics donate. Despite its seeming wealth, the Catholic Church doesn't have the money to present religious programming properly on television. For the last several years, the Vatican has had an annual deficit of over $30 million.

The myth of Catholic wealth works against an individual Catholic who wants to produce a program and buy time on popular stations. Because people think the church has so much money, there isn't an urgency to support Catholic television. Consciously or unconsciously, viewers think, "Oh, Father Smith doesn't need money as much as Jimmy Swaggart. Jimmy does not have the rich Catholic Church to bail him out if he runs into financial trouble."

The result of this way of thinking is that independent protestant evangelists can get a better financial response from viewers because they don't have a large church organization to help them when money is short. Until we can put to rest the idea that a Catholic on television has little need for support from viewers, Catholic television is never going to be the force it should be.

Should we work for unity with people of non-Christian religions?

Yes, as we struggle as individuals to reconcile

our faith with the church and the revelation of Jesus, we must remember that we have a great responsibility. We are called as Christ's followers to bring all people to God.

We have to face the fact that disunity among Christians is one of the major reasons non-Christians are not attracted to Christianity. Who would want to be a part of our bickering, prejudice, and even violence?

In the Gospel of John, Jesus prays that all may be one. That is an urgently important challenge to Christians today. If we are going to follow Jesus in His tireless drive to bring all people to Him and to His Father though Him, then we Christians have got to get our act together.

When I read the stories of Jesus' ministry in the Gospels, I find that He was tireless in His quest to bring all people to a love for His Father. Jesus is a lover, the greatest lover the world has ever known. True love is first directed to the other rather than to the self. Certainly, Jesus calls us to love Him, but He also wants us to direct our love to His Father. Would that we Christians could open a rich dialogue with people of non-Christian religions; a dialogue based on Jesus as the best example of how we can love the Father who is the God of Jews, Muslims, and Hindus.

Can you give an example of people who are doing this?

Not long ago when I had the privilege of traveling for three weeks in India, I was able to be with Mother Teresa for five days. My only contact with her in the past had been through television programs and books written about her. I got a good look at Christian missionary work among Hindus.

In India, as well as in most Muslim countries, Christians may not do direct proselytizing. Mother preaches Christ by caring for rejected and dying Hindus and Muslims.

My first meeting with Mother was in Bombay at a house called Asha Dan, which she founded for mentally and physically handicapped children. The neighborhood of this former factory contained some of the most subhuman living conditions I have ever seen. But Asha Dan was a haven of cleanliness, order, and joy. The day I came was a special one, for Mother Teresa was coming to help celebrate the home's thirteenth anniversary.

The first person to greet me at Asha Dan was a clean-cut American. I later learned that he was a professional tennis player, who had come to Bombay with his wife and child to give a year of his life in service to the boys and girls in Mother's home.

He brought me into a large building filled with physically handicapped children. I had to catch my breath as I saw the hundreds of sets of eyes that looked at me with silent, patient love. The tennis pro swooped up child after child in his arms, laughing with them and caressing them. These are children that no one had time for before Mother Teresa came into their lives. Now they receive love and medical care from Mother's Sisters, from doctors and many volunteers.

As we walked out the door I passed a changing room where Sisters and aides were busily preparing the children for the visit of Mother Teresa.

Outside, chairs had been set in rows before a stage where the formalities of the anniversary celebration were to be held. As I took my seat close to the front, I heard a little hum from the back—and then there was Mother Teresa, all three-feet-seven-inches of her, or so it seemed. In her white sari and faded gray sweater, she took a seat and then tried to ignore the photographers who formed a wall before her.

The program was simple and charming. We heard from a choir of the children and a famous Hindu singer. And there was a cake to be cut. Then the lady who had given me the trip to India, Joanne Petronella, put a beautiful statue of our lady of Fatima in my lap and told me to present it to Mother Teresa. I gulped but, at an appropriate moment, stood before Mother to give her the statue. Her wrinkled face looked up to me and then broke into a large smile. As I held her hand, I was struck by its softness and gentleness. I moved to the mike and spoke a few words of explanation and gratitude. I was awed by this simple woman who had so taken to heart Christ's words to love others, especially the poor and forgotten.

Then Mother was asked to say a few words. I have been told that she doesn't ordinarily speak too long. That day she waxed eloquent for some twenty-five minutes. She challenged us to love Jesus by loving others. This she said was the simple rationale for Asha Dan: love Jesus by loving the children that others want to forget.

This is the key to Mother's evangelizing in India. She isn't so concerned about preaching words about Jesus as I and other television evangelists do. She preaches Jesus by bringing his love to the forgotten and the despised. She puts Christ's words into radical action.

She had just returned from Russia where she had left some of her Sisters to care for needy people. She told a story of a woman she had met in Armenia after the earthquake. The woman had been pinned in a crumbled building for eight days. When she saw that the infant in her arms was going to die of hunger, she cut her finger and began feeding her baby with her own blood. When Mother Teresa saw the mother, she looked as if she weren't going to live, but the baby was the picture of health. "That's what real love is. That is like the love of Christ for us."

Two weeks later I flew across the country from Bombay to Calcutta, where on four successive mornings I was able to celebrate Mass with Mother and 350 of her Sisters, 300 of whom were young women in training to give their lives to Jesus as members of Mother's community, the Missionaries of Charity. As I stood at the altar, I was inspired. I don't know of any community of nuns in the States that can boast of three hundred novices.

The chapel was completely without decoration aside from a statue of Mary and a crucifix. The windows were all open. From the busy street below, the sounds of horns, streetcars, and trucks overwhelmed the gentle voice of a delicate Indian Sister, who in a British-Indian accent, proclaimed the Scriptures. I later learned that despite the sound interference, Mother wanted the windows left open so that the Sisters would be reminded that Christ's message is never to be isolated from the clatter of the world He loves.

Mother sat barefoot against the wall opposite the altar in this gigantic rectangular chapel. She had no place of honor among the sari-clad Sisters. Her only sign of distinction was that while the others wore faded blue sweaters, Mother's was a faded gray! Her humble insignificance in the chapel seemed incongruous given the fact that she was the winner of the Nobel prize and probably one of the best-known women in the world.

Aside from the longer talk she gave at Asha Dan when I first met her, she said next to nothing in the five times that I was with her. Oh, but she spoke volumes to my spirit. I am still trying to sort out her effects on my life.

Like her, I long for a revolution which will bring about a change from all the injustice, violence, and suffering in the world. With her I believe that Jesus' challenge of love is the simple answer to all the difficulties. I am awed by her radical surrender to Christ and His message. Could I let go, as she has done, of so many of the material comforts that seem so vital to me? Could I move toward caring for the people that frighten and repel me as she has done so completely?

My visit to India and Mother Teresa has had a profound effect on my life. She has placed in me a seed of challenge to let go of myself and trust God by loving others more unreservedly. I know that everything I say and do in the future will be colored by the people of India and Mother Teresa.

Mother's dedication to evangelization through love is the key to successful Catholic missionary work in the future.

SECTION 6

Conclusion

In the midst of pluralism and challenge, you have decided to remain Catholic. Can you explain?

When Jesus said at the Last Supper, "I will be with you always," He meant it. Not only would He speak to us in our hearts, He would also work through the church community to give us strength and direction, to keep us true to His revelation.

For me this Christian community is the Catholic Church. This church is important to me. In this Catholic community I find a spirituality that gives me direction in those problems we all share. In the midst of conflict of opinions and values that jab and push at me every day, I have found a haven of security and direction for my life. In the Catholic respect for diversity, I enjoy a freedom of worship and expression that I find enlivening. Despite its frequent rigidity and love for structure, I find an amazingly patient respect for criticism. I delight in how my community encourages me to see God's presence in people of other beliefs.

All of these generalities were formed through specific relationships with people in the Catholic Church.

First I think of my parents. I recall Mom sitting in a Catholic nursing home reading her large-print Bible and praying fervently for me and for the nurses who pestered her to go to God in prayer for them. Then there was Dad, who quietly fingered his rosary in the living room at our home in Pasadena.

The sixteen priests and brothers with whom I live in Riverside, California, are my most familiar experience of Catholicism. Brother John Carlucci is a vital part of that community. He lives across the hall from me. John is 94. He spent forty years as a missionary in the Philippines, including two years as a prisoner in a Japanese concentration camp. When he isn't beating me at chess, feeding his cats, and zipping around town on his motorcycle, he's sitting in front of the tabernacle in church five or six hours a day, praising God.

There are special Catholic friends and relatives whose love, laughter, and concern make Jesus real: Kelly Hanley, who honored me by asking me to give her first Holy Communion last year; Tom Sediva, who let me share with him the pain of his divorce; Philippus Herkata from Indonesia, whose generosity and devotion to Jesus gives me encouragement at moments of discourgement; and Billie Zabala, the ever-faithful friend whose kindness never seems to end.

Catholicism is the priests and seminarians I gave retreats to in Chicago, Denver, West Virginia, and Wisconsin. Catholicism is my local bishop, Phil Straling, whose love and enthusiasm for evangelization help to make a sometimes-intimidating church hierarchy an image of Christ.

Integral to my Catholic experience are the contemplative Sisters who pray for and support my television ministry: Mother Rose, Sister Gemma, Sister Margaret Mary, and the awesome Mother

Angelica with her national Catholic television network.

Thanks to the blessing of my television program, I am able to communicate my love for Jesus, as a Catholic, with thousands of people. The tender, needing, and encouraging letters from these friends have enabled me to keep the dream of Catholic television alive despite the continuing struggle for financial support.

With all of these positive influences, I'm not so naïve as to ignore weaknesses in certain individuals in the church. I am not so narrowminded that I don't realize that members and leaders in the church have been and still are sinners. The church is not made up entirely of saints. Once I face that fact, I can then struggle to strike the balance between Catholics who are outstanding examples of Christian life and other Catholics whose action or apathy is down right scandalous.

True to my understanding of faith, my commitment to Catholicism must be a continual quest to make the actions I perform and the people I follow conform to my understanding of Jesus and His revelation. I must also, with all humility, balance my personal understanding of Christ's revelation with the teaching of the church. And finally, I need to listen to people of other faiths and other Christian denominations to learn more about God's presence in the world. Oh, I find the prospect exhilarating!

Index

abandon 237
abortion 17, 18, 34, 71, 190, 195–202, 204, 216, 217
abstinence 134, 183
ACA 43, 44
Adam 120, 185
adultery 87, 126, 135, 149, 150
Advent 79
African-American 240
aging 70
agnostics 33
AIDS 16, 26, 60, 182–186
angel 92, 95, 96
Angelica, Mother 252
angels 10, 11, 81, 95
Anglican 231
Anglicans 228
annulled 139, 150, 151
annulments 34
Annunciation 88
anoint 119
anointing 172
Antichrist 12, 111, 112
antisemitism 232, 235
anti-Jewish 233
anxiety 38, 40, 96, 224
Apocalypse, the 12, 112
apparitions 10, 84, 85, 86
Aquinas, St. Thomas 50, 67, 134
Aramaic 94
Assumption of Mary, the 11, 53, 94, 95
atheistic 213
atheists 27, 33, 85
Augustine, St. 215, 234
Auschwitz 235

Baptism 12, 34, 65, 117–124, 142
Baptist 28, 118
baptize 12, 97, 118, 119, 122
beast 111
Beirut 110
Benedict 98
Benedictines 11, 98, 100
Bible 4, 8, 10, 18, 25, 31, 33, 37, 39, 49–58, 62, 68, 72, 76, 90, 92–95, 185, 203, 204, 231, 251
biblical 189, 235
birth control 70
blacks 239–241
blasphemies 111
Bolshevik 85
Boniface 238
Buddhism 231
Buddhists 27
bureaucracy 51

Calvin, John 56
canon 53, 62

canonization 11, 81, 82, 83
capitalism 213
capitalistic 238
cardinal 202
Carmelite 235
charism 63, 123
charismatic 12, 34, 76, 123, 124
charity 63
chastity 11, 82, 100, 182
chauvinistic 17, 200
Chrysostom, John 233, 234
church-hoppers 27
circumcised 170
clairvoyance 232
clergy 169
clericalism 50
clerics 51, 161, 168, 218
Communism 18, 211–214
condoms 16, 182–184
confession 12, 34, 126, 127, 128
confirmation 12, 86, 117, 118, 123, 124
conscience 139, 158, 162, 215, 216, 226, 230, 241
conservative 69, 169
contemplative 11, 100, 252
contraceptives 182, 183, 187
Corinthians 125, 165
crucifix 248
Cursillo 75

Dachau 110
deacons 160, 170, 243
demigod 94
demon 11, 96, 97
depressed 131, 225
devil 11, 54, 96–98, 232–234
dialogue 29, 30, 31, 75, 76, 90, 101, 142, 143, 149, 162, 182, 227, 228, 229, 231, 235, 236, 239, 245
diocese 97
discrimination 168, 169
divorce 14, 139, 142, 148, 149, 150, 151, 162, 191, 223, 252
doctrine 8, 61, 62, 95, 154, 155, 225, 227
dogmatically 112
dualologue 29
dying 16, 109, 121, 171, 190, 202, 246

Easter 61, 69, 142
Ecclesiasticus 56
ecumenism 155
emotion 42
emotional 110
Eucharist 13, 34, 57, 59, 64, 74, 76, 119, 136–138, 231
euthanasia 18, 202, 204

evangelization 20, 31, 99, 229, 239, 240, 241, 247, 249, 252
Exodus 55
exorcism 34, 96
exorcist 96, 97

Fatima 10, 84, 86, 247
forgive 13, 42, 43, 118, 129, 135, 167, 203
forgiven 13, 72, 119, 131, 132, 133, 172, 203, 224
forgiveness 7, 25, 43, 71, 109, 118, 123, 127, 128, 129, 131, 132, 135, 146, 167, 173, 185, 203, 220
forgiving 129, 132, 134, 135
Francis of Assisi, St. 98, 99, 238
Franciscans 11, 98
frozen embryo 17, 191, 192, 193
fundamentalists 20, 57, 243

Galatians 158
Galileo 155, 156
Gallup Poll 69
Gentile 170
Gentiles 42, 159
Greeley, Andrew 70
Greek Orthodox 161, 228
Gregory, Pope 234
Guadalupe 86, 242
guardian angels 11, 95, 96

Hebrew 31, 50, 56, 62, 77, 94, 111
Hebrews 56, 60, 209
heterosexual 181
hierarchy 15, 155, 160, 186, 218, 252
Hinduism 231
Hindus 20, 235, 245, 247
hispanics 20, 241, 242
holocaust 201
homily 50
homosexuality 16, 34, 103, 150, 181, 182, 184
hypocrites 28, 171, 146, 147

idolatry 79, 80, 126
Immaculate Conception 53, 155
immigrants 20, 106, 209, 240, 241
impotence 150
indulgences 19, 50, 225
Inquisition, the 15, 20, 158, 230
insemination 17, 186–188
intercession 81, 87, 89, 90, 92
intercommunion 230, 231
intercourse 16, 17, 135, 149,

180, 182, 188, 193, 196, 199
Israel 77, 234, 235

Janssenists 121
Janssen, Arnold 99
Japan 99
Japanese 252
Jerusalem 76
Jesuit 99
Jesuits 11, 99, 100
Jewish 25, 28, 77, 119, 146, 201, 234, 235
Jews 20, 27, 33, 34, 56, 78, 170, 217, 221, 226, 232–235, 238, 239, 242, 245
Judaism 234, 239
Judas 94, 234
judgmentalism 71
Junipero 238
justification 63

karma 232
Kingdom 74, 102, 111, 121, 154, 165, 173, 215, 217, 221, 222
Knights of Columbus 76

LARC 228
Lebanon 146, 236
Lefebvre, Archbishop 162, 163
Lenin 212
Lent 79
levitating 232
liberation theology 18, 209, 210, 211
limbo 12, 121, 122
Lourdes 86, 173
Lucifer 96, 232
Luther 51, 56, 99
Lutheran 30, 231
Lutherans 228

Maccabees 56
Magdalene, Mary 131
Magnificat, the 88
Mao Tse-Tung 212
Maronite Rite 227
Marx 212
Mary 33, 42, 81, 84–90, 92–95, 155, 173
masturbation 34, 199, 195
media 165, 166, 179, 182, 184, 194
meditation 41, 74, 92, 231
Melkite Rite 227
Methodist 28, 239
Methodists 228
miracles 16, 34, 81–86, 173, 174
mission 243
missionaries 20, 21, 99, 208, 237–242, 245, 249, 252
monologue 29
Muslim 221, 226, 246

Muslims 20, 27, 217, 235, 245
Mystical Body 108, 205, 206

Nicaragua 208
Nicodemus 129
Nirvana 232
Noriega, Manuel 209
Nostra Aetate 234

obedience 59, 82, 83, 101, 166, 177
occultism 232
ordination 97, 163, 169–171
origin 45
original sin 12, 119–121, 185
orthodox 31, 78

pain 108–110, 113, 162, 197, 205, 206
Palestine 56
papacy 15, 154–160
papal 15, 156, 159, 219
Passover 119
paternalism 103
penance 85, 126, 134, 225
Pentecostal 28
Pharisees 8, 62, 63, 133, 146, 147, 167
politics 18, 19, 70, 196, 201, 202, 207, 209, 215–219
pornography 34, 190, 193, 194
possession by demons 96
prejudice 160, 227, 236, 245
Presbyterian 173
priesthood 97, 118, 164–169, 241–242
pro-abortion 195, 198
pro-choice 19, 216
pro-life 19, 207, 217, 218
puritanical 180
Puritanism 194

rabbi 164, 228, 237
racism 186
racist 73, 240
rape 17, 196, 197, 200
rationalize 130
Redemption 170
remarriage 14, 149–151
remarrying 139
Revelation 95, 112

Sacraments 12, 14, 16, 34, 68, 74, 79, 81, 110, 115–129, 131, 133, 137, 139, 140, 166, 171, 172
sacred 9, 49, 52, 53, 76, 78, 115, 180, 183, 184, 188, 193
sacrifice 80, 82, 106, 118, 119
salvation 19, 20, 25, 33, 54, 63, 64, 93, 122, 134, 205, 206, 223, 224, 226, 229, 236, 237

Satan 11, 96, 97, 147, 158, 173
schism 161, 162
Screwtape Letters, The 98
scrupulosity 132
seamless garment 202
séances 90
seminarians 169, 242, 243, 252
seminaries 31, 50, 163, 240–243
Septuagint 56
sex 16, 71, 76, 82, 83, 102, 166, 179, 180, 181, 183, 184, 185, 190, 193, 194, 199
sexist 69, 169
sexual 16, 17, 34, 135, 149, 150, 166, 179–184, 186, 188, 189, 190, 194, 195, 196, 201
sexuality 16, 34, 104, 134, 179, 180, 181, 189–193
single-issue voter 18, 201
sister 10, 40, 43, 57, 61, 94, 157, 211, 235
Sisters 211, 246–248, 252
sperm 17, 189–191, 199
spirituality 33, 47, 50, 225, 232, 251
stockpile 186
stockpiling 214
surrogate parenthood 17, 188
symbols 79, 115, 119, 136, 161, 188

television (TV) 20, 129, 141, 183–185, 194, 243–245
Teresa, Mother 73, 245–249
test tube 193
test-tube baby 17, 188
tragedy 107, 108
transubstantiated 137
Trent, Council of 120, 137, 224
Trinity 53

unbaptized 121
unborn 192, 202, 216, 217
uncircumcised 159
unmarried 179
usury 156

vestments 9, 78, 79
Virgin (Mary) 11, 93, 94
virginity 53
vows 11, 59, 71, 82, 102, 166

war 84, 111, 202, 236, 240
women 16, 18, 143–146, 168–171, 187, 195–201, 216

Xavier, St. Francis 238

Yom Kippur 77